The Scent of Danger
A comedy
Michael Park

New Theatre Publications - London
www.plays4theatre.com

© 2013 BY Michael Park
First published in 2001

The edition published in 2013
New Theatre Publications
2 Hereford Close | Warrington | Cheshire | WA1 4HR | 01925 485605
www.plays4theatre.com   email: info@plays4theatre.com

New Theatre Publications is the trading name of the publishing house that is owned by members of the Playwrights' Co-operative. This innovative project was launched on the 1st October 1997 by writers Paul Beard and Ian Hornby with the aim of encouraging the writing and promotion of the very best in New Theatre by Professional and Amateur writers for the Professional and Amateur Theatre at home and abroad.

Rights of performance for NTP plays are controlled by New Theatre Publications, 2 Hereford Close, Warrington, Cheshire, WA1 4HR who will issue a performing licence on payment of a fee and subject to a number of conditions. These plays are fully protected under the Copyright Laws of the British Commonwealth of Nations, the United States of America and all countries of the Berne and Universal Copyright Conventions. All rights, including stage, motion picture, radio, television, public reading and translation into foreign languages are strictly reserved. It is an infringement of the copyright to give any performance or public reading of these plays before the fee has been paid and the licence issued. The royalty fee is subject to contract and subject to variation at the sole discretion of New Theatre Publications. In territories overseas the fees quoted in this catalogue may not apply. A fee will be quoted on application to New Theatre Publications.

The right of Michael Park to be identified as author of this work has been asserted by him in accordance with Section 77 of the Copyright, Designs and Patents Act 1988

ISBN 9 781 840 94932 2

Characters

Barry Bigley - *an incompetent private eye, 20s, tall slender*
Ethel Bigley - *Barry's mother, 50s, small, fussy, not very bright*
Sidney Bigley - *Barry's father, 50s, small dapper, energetic, educated*
Deirdre Fanshaw - *Barry's fiancée, 20s. short, dumpy, unfashionably dressed*
Luigi Salini - *Barry's landlord, 30-40s, Italian, mysterious*
Rick Connors - *Barry's mate, 20s, handsome, suave, sophisticated*
Suzanne Marchant - *a client, 20s, very attractive, rich, spoilt*
Gladys Cardoza - *a medium, 50s, theatrical, flamboyant*

Synopsis of scenes

ACT I Scene 1 - *a Monday evening in winter*
ACT I Scene 2 - *an hour later*
ACT I Scene 3 - *around midnight*
ACT II - *the following morning*

Copyright Information

The play is fully protected under the Copyright laws of the British Commonwealth of Nations, the United States of America and all countries of the Berne and Universal Copyright Conventions.

All rights including Stage, Motion Picture, Radio, television, Public Reading, and Translation into Foreign Languages, are strictly reserved.

No part of this publication may lawfully be reproduced in ANY form or by any means - photocopying, typescript, recording (including video-recording), manuscript, electronic, mechanical or otherwise - or be transmitted or stored in a retrieval system, without prior permission.

Licenses for amateur performances are issued subject to the understanding that it shall be made clear in all advertising matter that the audience will witness an amateur performance; that the names of the authors of the plays shall be included on all programmes, and that the integrity of the authors' work will be preserved.

The Royalty Fee is subject to contract and subject to variation at the sole discretion of New Theatre Publications.

In Theatres of Halls seating Four Hundred or more the fee will be subject to negotiation.

In Territories Overseas the fee quoted may not apply. A fee will be quoted on application to New Theatre Publications, London.

Video-Recording of Amateur Productions

Please note that the copyright laws governing video-recording are extremely complex and that it should not be assumed that any play may be video-recorded for whatever purpose without first obtaining the permission of the appropriate agents. The fact that a play is published by New Theatre Publications does not indicate that video rights are available or that New Theatre Publications control such rights.

The Scent of Danger

Performing Licence Applications

A performing licence for these plays will be issued by "New Theatre Publications" subject to the following conditions.

Conditions

1. That the performance fee is paid in full on the date of application for a licence.
2. That the name of the author(s) is/are clearly shown in any programme or publicity material.
3. That the author(s) is/are entitled to receive two complimentary tickets to see his/her/their work in performance if they so wish.
4. That a copy of the play is purchased from New Theatre Publications for each named speaking part and a minimum of three copies purchased for backstage use.
5. That a copy of any review be forwarded to New Theatre Publications.
6. That the New Theatre Publications logo is clearly shown on any publicity material. This is available on our website.

Fees

Details of script prices and fees payable for each performance or public reading can be obtained by telephone to (+44) 01925 485605 or to the address below.

Alternatively, latest prices can be obtained from our website www.plays4theatre.com where credit/debit cards can be used for payment.

To apply for a performing licence for any play please write to New Theatre Publications 2 Hereford Close, Warrington, Cheshire WA1 4HR or email info@plays4theatre.com with the following details:-

1. Name and address of theatre company.
2. Details of venue including seating capacity.
3. Dates of proposed performance or public reading.
4. Contact telephone number for Author's complimentary tickets.

Or apply directly via our website at www.plays4theatre.com

The Scent of Danger
by Michael Park

ACT I Scene 1

The scene is a small bedsit on the first floor of a block of flats in a small Northern town. It has been partly converted into a semblance of an office. At centre rear is a door, the top half of which is opaque and bears the backwards lettering 'IC INVESTIGATIONS'. A window is in wall L and is half open. Under this window is a small desk on which is an old-fashioned manual typewriter, a telephone and an answering machine, an angle poise lamp, empty In and Out trays, a pair of binoculars, a pair of stereo headphones, a games console joystick, some blank paper, cards with the office phone number on them, and a paper knife, pen and notebook. Under the desk is an empty waste paper bin, and down L of desk is a hat stand. A filing cabinet is at rear to L of door. Along wall R is a single bed with a bedside cabinet to R of door, carrying a small lamp, and an upright chair is at the front of the bed. C is a small coffee table on which is a neat pile of crime-type magazines. There are two exits DR and DL, which lead to the bathroom and kitchen respectively. The bed is covered by a counterpane and the room is spotless. As the Curtain opens, the stage is empty and the room is dark. There is light behind the glass door pane which is obscured by the shadow of a man. Then the door opens, and we see, framed in the light from the landing, the silhouette of BARRY BIGLEY. He wears a long beige raincoat and a trilby hat pulled down over his eyes. He stands for a moment, his hands thrust deep into his pockets, looking around the room, then reaches to the bedside lamp and switches it on. In the dim light, we can just make out that he is a young man, tall and slim. He closes the door and speaks in a deep voice with an American accent.

Barry Hank Silver stood perfectly still. His instincts, finely honed through years of dangerous investigations, told him that someone had been in the office recently. He sniffed the air. Yes, there was a faint aroma of perfume still lingering. He went through the filing cabinet that was his memory, analysing the scent, probing, searching for a name. Suddenly, he snapped his fingers. *(He tries to click his fingers and gives up after a few failed attempts.)* He thumped one fist into the palm of the other hand as recognition swept through him. Layla - the very name brought the perspiration to his brow and made his heart beat faster. Layla la Grande - one-time night club chanteuse and femme fatale - a girl who dabbled in everything illegal, yet whose innocent face could make you believe she was pure as the driven snow. Layla la Grande, the moll of

The Scent of Danger

Danny Devine, gangster and drug dealer. What would a girl like Layla want with a private eye? The question was going to haunt him until he found some answers. Maybe there was a message on the desk. Hank took off his well-worn hat and neatly hung it on the hatstand. *(He takes off his hat and hurls it towards the stand. It sails out of the window. In his normal, English voice.)* Oh, bloomin' heck! *(He moves to the desk. In American accent.)* Yes! There was a note with just two words - 'Help me'. Hank's brain processed the words at phenomenal speed. This could mean only one thing- Layla needed help! The paper still held a hint of her perfume. *(He takes a sheet of paper and holds it to his nose.)* And something else, something indefinable... the scent of danger! Suddenly, his keen ears picked up a faint sound. Someone was in the room! *(He moves away from his desk C.)* Hank glided like a panther towards the centre of the room, his every nerve-ending on alert. If there was to be any rough stuff, he knew he was in perfect physical condition, the result of hours of working out in the gym. He made sure his weight was evenly balanced so that he moved swiftly, silently and with deadly accuracy. *(He falls over the coffee table, picks himself up and hops around, clutching one foot. In his normal voice.)* Oh, me toe! *(He carefully places his foot on the ground and limps as he picks up any magazines which have been knocked from the table. He squares his shoulders and reverts to American.)* But it was just his fevered brain playing tricks. *(Another shadow appears on the glass door. Barry spins round.)* Suddenly, his heart stopped beating as he saw a shadow at the door. Who was it? Could it be Danny, come to settle old scores? Or could it be Layla herself, returning to pour her heart out in his willing arms?

(The door swings open to reveal Ethel. She is dressed in a flowered dress over which is a raincoat. Her hair is covered by a headscarf, and she is pushing a vacuum cleaner. She also carries Barry's hat. She switches on the overhead light.)

Ethel No it's your mother, come to give the place a clean. And I wish you'd get your landlord to get a lift fitted. It's not good for a woman my age to be climbing stairs.

Barry *(in his normal voice)* It's only one flight, mum. Anyway, I haven't seen my landlord since I signed the contract. Not that I want to. He's real creepy. Looks like a leftover from the days of prohibition.

Ethel *(peering round)* And who were you talking to? I hope you

ACT I Scene 1

haven't got a woman in here, our Barry. Our agreement when you left home was, no loose women.
Barry There are no women here, Mum , loose or fastened down. *(Takes off his raincoat and hangs it up.)*
Ethel Why are you limping like that?
Barry It's the usual way I limp.
Ethel I meant, what's up with you now? It was always something when you were young - grazed knees, cut lip, bubonic plague. If it was going around, you got it.
Barry *(pathetically)* I hurt my toe.
Ethel Do you want me to kiss it better?
Barry No thanks!
Ethel I always did when you were a bairn. And you fell for it every time and all. Good job too. It saved us a heck of a lot of expense buying medicines.
Barry I'll just sit down and rest it. *(Sits at the desk.)*
Ethel *(taking off her coat and scarf and hanging them on the stand)* And if there's no woman in here, who's this Akela I heard you talking to? Aren't you a bit old for the Cubs? Oh, and I found your hat in the gutter outside again. That's the third time this week. If you want to chuck it away, why don't you put it in the dustbin instead of littering the street? *(Hangs it on the stand.)*
Barry It's *Layla*, not Akela.
Ethel *(unwinding the vacuum cleaner flex)* They wouldn't have you in the Cubs when you were small. They said you were too ugly.
Barry They did not!
Ethel They did! Folks said I should keep you indoors, because you frightened all the other bairns. The only time I let you out was Hallowe'en, because you blended in with the others. And it was cheap, you not needing to wear any makeup.
Barry Mum!
Ethel Oh, it's true. Your Dad said we should take you back to the hospital and get a refund. But I said we were duty bound to give you a chance. Fortunately, you got better as time went on - not by much, but enough for us to decide to keep you.
Barry Thanks a million!
Ethel Don't mention it. Mind, if you hadn't improved by the time you were six, we were going to give you to the gypsies - that is, if the gypsies would have had you. They're a bit more choosy nowadays about what they take. Now, keep out of my way

	while I get on with my work.
Barry	Mum, you cleaned this place only yesterday.
Ethel	Then it's got at least twenty four hours of dust on it, hasn't it? And we don't want to start up your bronchial trouble, do we? I'm not going through all that again. Your Dad and me used to miss whole chunks of Coronation Street with you coughing and spluttering in the background. Still, I suppose you can't help having a weak chest. It goes with your weak chin. *(She holds up the mains plug.)* Where's your thingy?
Barry	Same place it was yesterday, by the door.
Ethel	You don't expect me to remember details like that, do you? *(She walks over to the door, bends down and then straightens up again.)* How many times do I have to tell you, Barry?
Barry	Tell me what?
Ethel	Just take a look here. *(Barry goes to look.)* What have I told you about these holes? You've got to block these holes, otherwise your electricity leaks out all over the room.
Barry	I keep forgetting. *(Returns to the desk.)*
Ethel	*(sniffing)* It's your funeral, son. And don't expect your Dad to go spending his redundancy money on flashy wreaths. You can make do with some daisies from the garden and like it. *(She plugs in the cleaner and then moves to Barry.)* Are you sure you're all right on your own, Barry, love? You know you're always welcome to come back and live with us. I've kept your old room just like it was.
Barry	Mum, I'm twenty two. I'm too old for Magic Roundabout wallpaper and Thomas the Tank Engine mobiles. *(He moves C.)* I like this place. It may not be much, but it's all mine - so long as I pay the rent. Which reminds me, I haven't lately. Al Capone will be sending his goons around.
Ethel	I used to like them Goons on the wireless. Your Dad said they were too daft to laugh at, but I thought what they got up to was very sensible.
Barry	Way before my time, Mum.
Ethel	If you're so desperate to pay the rent, you could always pay it to us. We could use a few extra bob now your Dad's out of work.
Barry	I'll give you some money when I start making some myself. I've only just got this business nicely underway. *(He wanders over to the bed and smooths the covers, his back to Ethel. Ethel picks up the binoculars and holds them to her eyes, looking out of the window.)* Of course, it's not Pinkerton's, but

	it's a start. And there are always going to be plenty of things to investigate, especially with the police being so understaffed. *(Ethel is having difficulty seeing, so she climbs onto the desk and points the binoculars out of the open window.)* And maybe, one day, the big one will come along - a divorce case, or even a kidnapping. That would be something, eh, Mum? Mum?
Ethel	She's at it again! I don't know how folks can do that sort of thing after a hard day's work. Your father and me never did that sort of thing, not even at night with the lights off. Well, I never! The brazen hussy is waving at me!
Barry	*(moving to her)* Mum! What are you doing? You'll get me arrested for being a Peeping Tom. It's a perfectly legitimate massage parlour. They're allowed to do things like that. *(He grabs the binoculars from her.)* And it's especially nice after a hard day's work.
Ethel	*(facing him)* Ee, our Barry! How do you know how nice it is? You haven't been in there, have you?
Barry	You needn't fret. You don't think I could afford their prices, do you?
Ethel	Oh, so you've enquired how much it is then?
Barry	Will you get down from there? You're putting footprints all over my papers.
Ethel	*(clambering down)* It's only mud - from when I took the dog out this morning.
Barry	We haven't got a dog now. She died last year.
Ethel	No, Barry. I distinctly remember throwing the ball for her to fetch. Only she didn't... fetch it, I mean. She just ran away down Hartmore Street.
Barry	That's probably because she belongs to someone living down there. You keep taking *other peoples*' dogs for walks!
Ethel	That explains why it didn't come back when I shouted 'Rover'. Oh well, I'll try again tomorrow. Hey up! You've got a phone. *(Picks it up and listens.)*
Barry	Put it down. It was only installed this afternoon, and I don't want it broken.
Ethel	I'll be able to call you for a chat.
Barry	From the call box? That'll cost a bit. You don't have a phone at home.
Ethel	You're right. Still a face to face call is better than using one of them things. They always make me sound like Mr Punch. Now, what was I doing?

The Scent of Danger

Barry Just going, perhaps?
Ethel Ee, have I finished hoovering already? Take note, our Barry. See how quickly you can do things when you're organised. *(She crosses and unplugs the hoover.)* And how many times have I told you about these holes?
Barry *(wearily)* I'll get some covers for the sockets.
Ethel I'll knit you some. I think I've got some cream wool left over from when I knitted that coat for the dog. Typical of animals, that is. I was cross! I slaved over that coat so it'd be ready for the winter and what does that dog do? She drops down dead just after I've finished it. They've no gratitude, dogs. Not like goldfish.
Barry Goldfish don't show gratitude.
Ethel They do, you know. Every time I feed Jaws, he wags his little tail like crazy.
Barry *(crossing to hatstand)* Here's your coat.
Ethel Have I dusted already?
Barry You have.
Ethel Just goes to show, Barry, these doctors know nowt.
Barry How do you make that out?
Ethel They say you slow down as you get older. But I'm living proof you speed up. Look how quickly I did this room.
Barry Yes. You're brilliant, Mum. I'll see you later.
Ethel *(coiling up the hoover flex)* So you're not coming home?
Barry I *am* home. *This* is my home. Look, bed, chair, through there *(Pointing DR.)* bathroom. Through there *(Pointing DL.)* kitchen.
Ethel *(looking around)* I don't see a wife.
Barry I'm not getting married yet. I haven't found the right girl.
Ethel Have you tried growing a beard?
Barry Why should I want to grow a beard?
Ethel Well, it'd hide a goodly bit of your face. A pair of sunglasses, and your hat pulled well down, and you'd be halfway presentable.
Barry Will you stop insulting me? I thought mothers were supposed to care for their offspring.
Ethel Oh, we do, son, we do. But I bet I'm not the only mother who wishes she'd produced something bonnier to make all that pain worthwhile. Of course, there's always that Deirdre, but I'm sure even you could do better.
Barry She's all right, is Deirdre.

ACT I Scene 1

Ethel I suppose at least she doesn't scream with fright when she claps eyes on you.
Barry Goodbye, mother.
Ethel Am I going?
Barry You certainly are.
Ethel I've got to wait for your Dad. He dropped me off while he went to the library.
Barry He's still researching, then?
Ethel He's got to, Barry. He's got to read and read if he wants to succeed. Ooh, I'm a poet!
Barry There's no money to be made in TV quiz shows. Even if you win, you just get a vase or some such with your name on it.
Ethel Your Dad reckons it's not the winning, it's the appearing. He reckons everyone who appears on tele' seems to live in a big house and drive a flash car. He reckons once them tele' people set eyes on him, he's going to be snapped up. He fancies doing a programme like that Killjoy feller. He'll be good at that, would your Dad. Interviewing people.
Barry Come off it, Mum! He never listens to anyone else's opinion. He's too keen for everyone to hear his.
Ethel Anyroad, he reckons the way in is through these quiz shows, so he's going to learn as much as he can. *(A shadow appears at the door, followed by a knock.)* That'll be him now.
(Barry opens the door to admit Sidney. He is a brisk, no-nonsense Northerner in his fifties, wearing a flat cap, collarless shirt, jacket, and corduroy trousers.)
Sidney *(angrily)* Right across the pavement! Would you credit it? Right across the pavement outside here! I had to step into the road to avoid it. Take my life in my hands because some inconsiderate, jumped-up wazzock...
Ethel I know, dear. Some people never clean up after their dogs. I always picked up after ours. Mind, I didn't half get through some pairs of gloves.
(During the following, Ethel does some dusting, pushing Barry and Sidney aside as she rushes around.)
Sidney Not dog muck, Ethel. A ruddy caravan! Not content with taking up half the road, they've now taken to parking them on the pavements! And where are the traffic wardens, eh? Like the police in this town - never around when you want them. But you stop your car for five seconds on a double yellow, and , miracle of miracles, you're suddenly surrounded by half the cast of 'The Bill'!

The Scent of Danger

Barry Evening, Dad.
Sidney *(suddenly noticing him)* Oh, evening, Barry. You want to get onto the Council about that.
Barry About the police never being around when you want them?
Sidney No! About that caravan. Folk could injure themselves badly if they walked into it without seeing it.
Barry It's bad for blind people, I admit, Dad. But otherwise you'd have to be a right idiot to walk into something that big. *(He laughs.)* A real plonker.
Sidney *(menacingly)* I did.
Barry *(his laughter ceasing)* Yes, well... I didn't mean...
Sidney I was thinking of something else at the time, something more important than ruddy caravans. I was wondering how many countries are in the European Community at present.
Barry Well, yes, you would, wouldn't you.
Sidney It's amazing how much knowledge is stored away in that library. Reams and reams of fascinating facts. Did you know, Barry, that Carlisle's in Cumbria? Or that Victor Hugo wrote 'Les Miserables'? *(He pronounces it phonetically.)* And I always thought it was Julian Lloyd Rice wrote it.
Barry Knowing that sort of thing doesn't stop you walking into caravans, though.
Sidney I've never had much time for caravanners. Your Uncle Billy used to have one. He pulled it along with a Hillman Imp, so you can imagine what speed he reached - twenty maximum and that downhill with the wind behind him.
Barry That car was clapped out.
Sidney It was by the time it had pulled those two, plus a caravan, all round Scotland. Not only did he cause major traffic jams, but he was always forced to camp wherever he broke down. If I had my way, caravan owners'd pay ten times the road tax! And as for that one outside, I'd fine him - fine him a hundred pounds for every foot it stuck out onto the pavement!
Barry You don't have to worry. It's probably going soon. I think it belongs to the people in the flat below this one. They're flitting at the moment
Sidney *(thoughtfully)* I wonder if I'd ever get asked a question on the number of caravans on the roads today? I must contact the AA. Oh, what it is to possess knowledge, son! Why, when I think of that pathetic education I had...
Ethel Failed his eleven-plus, did Sidney. His mother was ever so

	proud.
Barry	Proud he failed to get into grammar school?
Ethel	It meant he didn't have to wear that awful green and yellow school uniform. Never could bear green with yellow, couldn't your Gran.
Sidney	But not now, Ethel. Now I'm a storehouse of information. Go on. Try me out!
Barry	Dad, I've got work to do...
Sidney	You've time for your Dad, haven't you? *(He turns the desk chair around and points the angle poise lamp at it, then sits.)* Go on, Ethel.
Ethel	What do you want me to do, Sidney?
Sidney	Be Magnus Magnusson.
Ethel	Oh, I don't think I could do that, not even if I knew what it was.
Sidney	He's not an 'it, Ethel, he's a 'who'. He's a quizmaster.
Ethel	But I'm not a master, I'm a Mrs.
Sidney	Just ask me my name.
Ethel	I know full well who you are! We've been married nigh on thirty years.
Sidney	*(wearily)* Ask me anyhow.
Ethel	Oh, all right. What's your name, Sidney?
Sidney	Not like that, like this - 'Name?'
Ethel	Why, you know my name. It's Ethel Bigley.
Sidney	Occupation?
Ethel	Looking after a layabout.
Sidney	You're not entering into the spirit of this, are you? Barry, take over.
Barry	Do I have to?
Sidney	You'd like to see your old Dad winning 'Mastermind', wouldn't you?
Barry	It'd be a miracle if you did. The programme finished ages ago.
Sidney	Did it? I thought old Magnus was just taking a break. Oh, well, it'll have to be 'Fifteen to One' then.
Barry	Fifteen? There are only three of us. And one will have to ask the questions.
Sidney	It'll be a mini version. Barry, put that chair in the corner and stand behind it. *(Barry takes the upright chair DR, reverses it and stands behind it.)* I'll stand behind this one. *(He reverses the chair and stands behind it.)* Ready when you are, Ethel... I mean Mr Stewart.

The Scent of Danger

Ethel My name's not Stewart, it's Bigley. You'll not get far on quizzes if you can't remember your family name.
Sidney That's the name of the quizmaster.
Ethel I thought it was Magnet Magnetism.
Sidney That was another quiz .
Ethel I'm getting confused now.
Barry Join the club!
Ethel I haven't got any questions.
Sidney Make some up, woman!
Ethel *(frantically looking around)* Er, er... what's written on that door?
Sidney Ye Gods! We're not playing I-Spy, Ethel! General knowledge questions.
Ethel I don't think I know anything about generals.
Sidney Go stand in the corner.
Ethel Do I have to, Sidney? I've not been that naughty have I?
Sidney It's not because you've been naughty, you daft... Take Barry's place. *(Ethel and Barry swop places.)* Barry, take over before I forget everything I've ever learned.
Barry Fifteen to One with two people - whatever next!
Sidney At the end of the contest, it's often down to two people. Which shows how much you know! First question, please.
Barry Oh, all right. Who works at Number Eleven, Downing Street?
Sidney Easy. The Chancellor of the Exchequer. I nominate Ethel.
Barry What's that mean?
Sidney *(patiently)* When I get a question right, I can pass the next one to my opponent. Go on, ask your mother one.
Barry *(sighing)* What *am* I doing here?
Ethel I know that one! You live here! Dominate Sidney!
Sidney That wasn't a general knowledge question.
Ethel It was. Everyone in the family knows Barry lives here. I told them, so that makes it general knowledge!
Sidney I give up! Here I am, trying to make the name of Bigley world famous, and what help do I get? Athletes get top quality coaching, boxers get first-class sparring partners, tennis teams are given hours to practise to get themselves into tip-top condition. What do I get? A dotty woman with a fetish for vacuum cleaners, and a son who thinks he's Mickey Spillane. Don't you want me to be successful?
Barry Of course we do, Dad. We're proud of the way you've come

ACT I Scene 1

from nothing...
Sidney I hope you don't mean that, son. The 'come from nothing' bit. I'll have you know I was the best cat's eyes maintenance engineer the Council ever employed. It wasn't some fly-by-night job, you know. On my skills depended the lives of thousands, nay millions of motorists throughout North Yorkshire. Best invention ever, the cat's eye, lad, and invented by a Yorkshireman. And I can tell you, I knew them cat's eyes inside out and back to front.
Barry Wouldn't it have been better to have known them the right way round?
Sidney You may scoff, Barry, but I lighted the way home for motorists for most of my life. And what thanks did I get? They gave the job to a younger man - said I was getting too old to do the bending. And after thirty years service, do you know what they presented me with?
Barry Yes, Dad. It's acting as a door stop in your living room.
Sidney A gold-painted cat's eye, that's what they gave me. And in the Chief Executive's speech, he couldn't even remember my name. I've gone down in the annals of Council history as Sidney *Bogley*! I sound like something your mother keeps cleaning!
Barry We were all very sorry how they treated you, Dad.
Sidney So you see, Barry, I've got to prove myself. I've got to show them what I'm made of. And I need all the help I can get. It's a matter of pride for the whole Bogley family... I mean, *Bigley* family.
Barry I'm sure you'll get on the tele' one day, Dad.
Sidney If I don't, it won't be for lack of trying. *(He looks around.)* You done, Ethel? This place may not be much to look at, son, but it's clean, thanks to your mother.
(Ethel puts on coat and scarf.)
Barry Yes, and I'm very grateful.
Sidney Not grateful enough to make sure she doesn't have to negotiate a damn great caravan on her way in! Give me that hoover, Ethel. We'll be on our way. *(He takes the vacuum cleaner.)* You know, Barry, you want to find yourself a nice girl and get wed.
Barry It's good of you to think about me, Dad.
Sidney Not for you - for *me*! Then I'll get your mother back. I never get my meals on time since your mother started coming round here at all hours cleaning up after you. Mind, I doubt all you'd

The Scent of Danger

          ever attract are short-sighted women.

Barry   What about Deirdre?

Sidney   Proves my point. I'm sure she wasn't wearing her glasses when she first met you. By the time she'd dug them out, put them on and seen what you really looked like, it was too late. After you, Ethel. And mind out for that caravan!
(Ethel waves to Barry as she exits, followed by Sidney.)

Barry   *(calling after them)* That's just what a lad needs to boost his self-confidence- supportive parents. *(The door closes behind them. Barry goes back to the desk and turning his chair round, resumes his American accent.)* Hank relaxed and let his brain go into freewheel. And naturally it immediately returned to Layla - Layla la Grande - even the name was poetry. Her image formed in his mind; the sheen of her hair as it fell in soft waves to her waist, black as the night sky; the milky whiteness of her smooth skin; her slender figure and those long legs which seemed to go on forever. And not forgetting those eyes, piercing blue, shining with love and passion. She spoke, and the sound of her voice was like music from the stars...
(The door bursts open and Deirdre staggers in. She is burdened down with carrier bags full of shopping which she drops on the floor. She appears short and dumpy; and wears large spectacles. Her hair is mousy and styled in an unflattering bun. She wears a fawn duffel coat, bright scarf, and a woolly hat. Underneath the coat, she wears a baggy jumper and a plain skirt. She is very 'Yorkshire' and very loud.)

Deirdre Hey up, sweetheart! Ee, I'm fed up with shopping. Town's like a madhouse. And who put that damn great caravan on the pavement? I walked smack into it! *(Takes off her coat and scarf and throws them on the bed.)*

Barry   Hello, Deirdre.
(Deirdre crosses to Barry and plonks down on his knee, eliciting a groan from Barry. She throws her arms round him and kisses him noisily. Barry struggles, but she has him in a tight grip.)

Deirdre And how's my big brave private eye today eh? How many cases has my clever boy friend solved so far? How many grateful citizens of Welham have lined up in this very office to shake your hand in congratulation - and cross your palm with silver?

Barry   Er, not a lot.

Deirdre Come on, Barry. Don't be bashful. How many? Four? Five?

ACT I Scene 1

	Any juicy cases, eh? You know, you're ever so lucky being your own boss. Not like us lesser mortals who have to do menial tasks to make ends meet. Come on! Is it five?
Barry	A bit less than five.
Deirdre	How many less than five?
Barry	Oh, around five less.
Deirdre	Oh well, never mind. There's always tomorrow, as my mum says.
Barry	She always was strikingly original, was your mother.
Deirdre	It's just that people haven't got around to finding where you are yet. You've only been going a little while. And I still love you.
Barry	That's nice to know.
Deirdre	You know, Barry, you look all sort of misty today, sort of like them actresses in them old movies. You know, when they filmed them through that gauze stuff to make them look more romantic. That's just what you look like - romantic.
Barry	*(gloomily)* Your glasses are misted up.
Deirdre	*(removing her glasses and wiping them on her sleeve)* So they are. I must be going senile. I hate having to wear glasses. Do you think I should get contacts, Barry? Would you still fancy me as much in contacts? *(She gets up and does a twirl in front of him.)* Do you think they'd fit in with my overall fashion style?
Barry	You'd still look fashionable in a gas mask.
Deirdre	I'll tell you one thing about contacts, Barry. They wouldn't get in the way when we were snogging, like specs do. *(She plonks down on his knee again, making him gasp for breath.)* Do you know what was going through my mind while I was battling through the crowds in the supermarket?
Barry	Mars bars? Crisps? Chocolate?
Deirdre	Not food, silly! I was thinking about you. Were you thinking about me?
Barry	Oh yes, of course. Hardly a minute goes by without me thinking about you.
Deirdre	Is that right? Ooh, that makes me go all warm inside.
Barry	Are you sure that's not the pizza?
Deirdre	How did you know I had pizza?
Barry	Just an inspired guess - plus the fact that you always have a pizza every time you go shopping.
Deirdre	I've got to keep up my strength, haven't I?
Barry	It's not your strength that worries me. Could you get up?

The Scent of Danger

You're crushing me.

Deirdre *(getting up)* All right then. How about us... you know.
Barry Sorry, I don't know.
Deirdre Us having a bit of a lie-down - on the bed.
Barry I'm not tired.
Deirdre No! *You* know. A bit of a cuddle. We won't go too far though. I'm saving myself till we get married. We are still getting married, aren't we, darling?
Barry That may not be for some time. For a start, I need to make loads of money...
Deirdre For that cottage in the country, eh? With the nursery for little Wayne and little Sharon. And you won't forget to fit a catflap, will you, for Tiddles?
Barry I've got it on my list.
Deirdre Well then?
Barry Well then what?
Deirdre How about a cuddle?
Barry I'm sorry, Deirdre, but I'm just about to start this very important case.
Deirdre What important case? There's nothing in your in-tray.
Barry *(jumping up)* Ah, well... it was... it was a phone message, that's it! This bloke phoned and wanted me to look into... look into... er, his wallet!
Deirdre And what did you expect to see? Credit cards, maybe? Some money, perhaps?
Barry Not 'look into' as in 'look in to'. 'Look into' as in 'investigation'. It's been pinched and he wants me to find it.
Deirdre How exciting! Have you any clues?
Barry I've got to dash out and find some right away.
Deirdre If it's only a wallet, then it will keep for a few more minutes. Now, if it were a child being kidnapped, or maybe a cat, then that would be important. There's been a lot of cat-napping going on round our way lately.
Barry I don't have time to go running after missing cats. I'm here to investigate serious crimes.
Deirdre Do you mean to say that if our Tiddles went missing, you wouldn't go and look for him? You know, Barry Bigley, you have a cruel streak in you.
Barry As there is no Tiddles, the question doesn't arise, does it? And I'd have to be pretty desperate to take a job which involved sneaking down back alleys looking for useless heaps of four-

legged fur!
Deirdre You're making me look at you with new eyes, Barry.
Barry That's because your glasses aren't misted up any more.
Deirdre Oh, what the heck! You're still my Barry deep down. Come on, sweetheart. Give us a cuddle. You would if you loved me.
Barry *(allows himself to be led to the bed.)* Like a lamb to the slaughter.
(Deirdre takes him in a bear hug and falls on top of him on the bed. Barry lies there, winded, his arms flailing. Enter Rick Connors. He is in his twenties, suave, sophisticated and self confident. He wears a smart suit and tie.)
Rick Oops! Sorry about this, old mate. Wrong moment entirely. *(He speaks to someone outside.)* Come on, doll, we'll go for a walk until they come up for air.
Barry *(struggling from underneath Deirdre)* No! Rick! Come back! We weren't doing anything.
Rick It didn't look like nothing from where I was standing.
Barry Honest. We were just, er, testing the springs.
(Deirdre gets up but has lost her glasses. She bends over the bed, feeling around blindly.)
Rick I think she's looking for you, old son.
Deirdre Glasses, Barry! I can't find my glasses!
Rick No need to stand on ceremony with friends, Deirdre. We'll do without the glasses. We'll drink out of the bottle.
Barry They're here. *(He hands the glasses to Deirdre and moves to Rick.)* Nice to see you.
Rick I've brought someone to meet you. Come on in, love.
(Suzanne Marchant enters confidently. She is a very attractive young woman, dressed fashionably and obviously well-off.)
Rick Barry, Deirdre, I'd like you to meet the lovely Suzanne.
Barry *(gasping)* Good grief - Layla!
Rick You what?
Barry Sorry, I said, er…li-lo. The mattress is a li-lo. That's why we were testing it… to see it didn't burst when a heavy weight fell on it! *(He takes Suzanne's hand and gazes adoringly at her.)* Hello!
Rick Lucky you had Deirdre on hand then. For the heavy weight.
Deirdre Do you mind! I'm on a diet.
Barry *(babbling)* It's called the pizza diet. You order a pizza to be delivered, then move house before it arrives. Saves on food, but costs the earth in new curtains and carpets.

The Scent of Danger

Rick Barry, you're burbling.
Suzanne And could I have my hand back, please?
Barry Oh, sorry. I'm sorry. I didn't mean... er, this is my... my... this is Deirdre.
Deirdre *(with total lack of enthusiasm)* Hello. I'm Barry's fiancée - for the time being.
Barry Do sit down.
(He frantically brushes the seat of the desk chair with his hand. Suzanne moves towards the desk chair, but Deirdre nips in first and sits on it. Barry moves the upright chair for Suzanne to sit on, then hovers near her.)
Rick *(throwing himself on the bed)* So, Barry, how's business?
Barry Fine, fine. Rushed off my feet.
Rick You know, when you said you were setting up as a private eye, I must admit I had my doubts. After all, when we saw that bloke from the Job Centre when we left school, he wasn't exactly enthusiastic about your prospects.
Barry *(laughing in embarrassment)* Rubbish! It wasn't that bad. All he said was that I was just the teeniest bit unemployable, that's all. Anyway, what sort of job is mini-cabbing? You're out all hours, in all weathers, having to tug your forelock to the great British public.
Rick It does have its perks, and it just so happens you're unable to take your eyes off the current perk.
Suzanne I'm not sure I like being referred to as a 'perk'.
Barry *(adoringly)* Oh, but you are! A lovely perk... perky, you seem very perky! And what is that perfume you're wearing?
Suzanne This? It's called 'Dangerous'. It retails at forty pounds a bottle.
Barry It's very heady.
Deirdre Don't you like mine, Barry? It costs one pound fifty at Superdrug.
Suzanne What's it called -'Keep Your Distance'?
Rick Now, now girls!
Suzanne Rick tells me you've been friends for a long time, Barry.
Barry Oh ages and ages - not that I'm that old, you understand!
Deirdre We all went to school together, didn't we, *darling?*
Barry School, yes, that was it.
Rick Best friends since infants, right Bas?
Deirdre You were not! You used to make his life hell, the poor darling! You used him as the butt of your stupid jokes from the time his mother left him crying at the school gate.

ACT I Scene 1

Barry *(to Suzanne, smiling idiotically)* I was fifteen at the time, but emotionally immature.
Rick I think you're exaggerating a bit there, Deirdre. Sure I put the occasional pet mouse down his trousers...
Deirdre That was no mouse! It was a great rat! It's a miracle the experience didn't warp him for life.
Suzanne It's a miracle its *teeth* didn't warp him for life!
Barry It wasn't all bad. In fact, when I walked round the playground with it wriggling away down there, the girls seemed quite impressed.
Deirdre Rick was the school bully and he loved picking on weaklings like Barry.
Barry Er, I wouldn't say I was exactly a weakling...
Deirdre Just because he had a bad chest and his mother made him wear two pullies and a vest.
Suzanne Poor Barry! How you must have suffered.
Barry Oh, I did, I did.
Rick That wasn't the worst. She also made him go to school in a woolly balaclava helmet.
Barry Lots of the kids wore balaclavas.
Rick But you wore yours back to front with two eye holes cut in it so you could see where you were going. We never did make out why. It was almost as though she thought you were too ugly to be seen out.
Barry I had very delicate skin. It was so the cold didn't get at my face.
Rick In mid-summer?
Deirdre See? You're picking on him again. Never you mind, Barry. I stood up for you then, and I'll go on doing it.
Barry Yes, come to think of it, Rick, you picked on Deirdre as well.
Rick That wasn't me. That was Big Donna.
Barry Your partner in bullying.
Rick She went her own way, believe me. All she did was point out the fact that Deirdre was the only girl in school that the lads paid good money to so she *wouldn't* show them her knickers behind the bike sheds!
Suzanne Charming as your reminiscences undoubtedly are, could we get to the point of this visit?
Rick Sure, doll. You'll be dead chuffed when you hear this, Barry. We've got a job for you.
Barry A job?

The Scent of Danger

Rick Yes. You know what one of those is, don't you?
Barry Of course. I'm out every day, pounding the pavements...
Rick *(getting to his feet)* Save your breath. Anyone can see you're not exactly snowed under. Otherwise you wouldn't have time to be lying low on your li-lo with Deirdre. Suzanne has encountered a small problem which needs investigating. So naturally I thought of you.
Deirdre Oh, I get it! You'll be raking in a commission!
Rick *Au contraire,* Deirdre. That's French, by the way. Any money Suzanne cares to put Barry's way is all his - and the Inland Revenue's naturally. And I should point out at this stage, seeing as you haven't recognised her already, that Suzanne is one of the Tollerbay Marchants.
Deirdre I'd have put her down more for a 'marchant' seaman!
Barry You don't mean the people that own Snaresby Manor, that massive house in York Road?
Rick The same. Her father owns Knebleys, the international diamond company. He is what you call 'well-off'. And you might have seen Suzanne in her other role, Deirdre. You look the type who buys her clothes from catalogues. Well, Suze here is one of their top models.
Deirdre Appears in the children's section, does she? And if she's rich, she could have the pick of any man in the country. So, what's she doing with you?
Rick Better ask her that, hadn't you? I just happened to get a call to transport her to a modelling session out of town a few weeks ago, we got talking, and found we had a lot in common.
Deirdre And they don't come much more common than you!
Rick Really Deirdre, you ought to curb that sarcastic tongue of yours. You could drive business away from your boyfriend if you treat potential customers to that poisonous wit. Anyway, Barry, do you want the job or not? You're not the only private eye in town.
Deirdre No, but he's probably the cheapest.
Rick I told you money was no object.
Deirdre *(getting to her feet)* Don't give me that. I'm not stupid. The reason rich people stay rich is that they don't go chucking their money about.
Suzanne You're really quite sharp, Deirdre.
Deirdre Yes, well, my mother always says I've just climbed out of the knife box.

ACT I Scene 1

Suzanne *(smiling sweetly)* Accommodation at your house a little cramped is it?
Deirdre If I were you, I'd tell her what to do with her job, Barry.
Barry Hold on a minute! I do need the work, I admit.
Deirdre But he doesn't take on rubbish. As a matter of fact, at this very moment, he should be out searching for a wall...
Barry *(hastily)* Wallaby! It's gone missing from the zoo.
Rick I didn't hear about that.
Barry They don't want to alarm people.
Suzanne Maybe you could combine the two jobs. I've lost an animal too.
Deirdre Your mink coat made a dash for freedom, has it?
Suzanne As a matter of fact, it's my pet cat. I call her Cleopatra.
Deirdre I knew it wouldn't be something simple, like Patch! And I think you ought to know that Barry doesn't consider missing cats important enough to waste time on...
Barry Of course they are! Why, pets are part of the family, aren't they? I'm sure you're terribly upset, Miss, er, Miss... Suzanne. I cried for a week when our dog died.
Deirdre You only cried because your mother used to share its biscuits with you as a treat.
Barry *(quickly)* She always bought it ordinary biscuits, not the doggy ones.
Suzanne *(getting to her feet and placing her hands on his)* I'm *so* glad to have found someone who understands so well. Now, Cleo's black, with the cutest little white patch on her nose. *(She touches Barry's nose.)* One ear bent over *(She touches Barry's ear)*, and she has one white paw, left front *(She touches his hand.)* And she's been spayed...
Deirdre *(pulling Barry away)* Yes, well I don't think he needs to be shown where *that* little operation took place!
Suzanne And her name is on her collar. Do you know, Barry, I can somehow sense that Cleopatra's future is in the safest of hands.
Barry *(breathing hard)* Oh, it is, Suzanne!
Suzanne Is it all right if he takes the job in hand, Deirdre?
Deirdre Just so long as his hands stay well away from you!
Rick I bet his hands have the safety catch permanently on when you're around, Deirdre. You and fun were never exactly bosom mates.
Deirdre Did you hear that, Barry? He insulted me!
Barry *(gazing adoringly at Suzanne)* Did he? Oh good!

The Scent of Danger

Suzanne Come on, Rick, I think we can leave everything to Barry.
Rick Righto. Give Suze a bell at the Manor if you come up with anything. To the salon, then, gorgeous.
Suzanne I'm having an aromatherapy session. I find them so relaxing, and very useful when you have to face up to the daily rigours of life, don't you agree, Deirdre?
Deirdre I'm still trying to work out what sort of rigours *you* meet each day.
Suzanne Oh, being rich isn't all it's cracked up to be. Sometimes, I just *yearn* to be ordinary- a bit like you, Deirdre. You don't realise how lucky you are.
Deirdre Oh, yeah, when I'm flogging away behind a supermarket checkout, I often think to myself, 'You want to count your blessings you weren't born rich, Deirdre'. If I was I'd be missing out on all this wonderful social contact with the caring, considerate, patient, smiling, friendly Great British Public.
Suzanne Ooh, you're so tense! You ought to try this aromatherapy treatment. Do you know Hattie's, behind the supermarket? She often stays open late, just for little me.
Deirdre (*in a fake posh voice*) To tell the truth, I'm hin and hout of there like a ferret up a trouser leg.
Suzanne There's no need to be like that. In fact, you might like to join me some time.
Deirdre (*sweetly*) Why? Are you coming apart?
Suzanne Come on, Rick. There's no talking to her. You can have a drink at the pub while you're waiting for me. Hope you don't mind if I'm a *teeny* bit late. When Hattie and I get reminiscing about Roedean, we never know when to stop.
Deirdre Oh, I know how it is! Me and me mates are the same about Canal Road Infants!
Suzanne (*she holds out a set of car keys*) I'll let you drive me there as a small favour.
Barry Haven't you got your cab tonight, Rick?
Rick I'm off-duty, old son, and Suze does have a Porsche. Does my street cred no end of good to be seen driving it even a short distance.
Suzanne Bye, Deirdre. So nice meeting you.
Deirdre The feeling was definitely *not* mutual!
Barry Goodbye Suzanne. I'll get on to it right away.
Suzanne Fine, but don't forget your wallaby, will you?
Barry What wallaby? Oh *that* wallaby. Cleopatra takes top priority,

believe me.
Suzanne *(kissing him on the cheek)* I just knew she would. Bye.
Rick So long, Barry. We'll have to get together for a pint sometime.
Barry Sure. *(Shows Suzanne and Rick out, then returns, closing the door behind him.)*
Deirdre *(mimicking)* 'Cleopatra takes top priority, believe me'! I'm surprised at you, Barry, getting all steamed up over a woman whose only claim to fame is her Daddy's wealth. And what happened to your distaste at having to sneak down back alleys looking for four-legged balls of fur?
Barry I need the money, simple as that.
Deirdre You'll get a reward for finding the wallet, won't you?
Barry Ah, yes, the wallet.
Deirdre You'll have no difficulty in recognising it when you spot it - apparently it's in the shape of a wallaby.
Barry I had to say that. You don't want Rick knowing I'm having to take on any old work, do you? Right! I must get moving.
Deirdre What about our cuddle?
Barry Sorry, Deirdre, no time for that sort of thing now. I've got to get out there, on the mean streets. *(He adopts an American accent.)* There's a tidal wave of crime threatening to engulf us out there. And it's up to people like me to make sure that little old ladies can walk the pavements in safety...
Deirdre You're looking for a missing cat, not taking on the Mafia single-handed!
Barry A cat now, a serial killer tomorrow. Deirdre, make way for Barry Bigley - crime-stopper. *(Walks to the hat stand and gets in a terrible tangle putting on his coat. Deirdre goes and helps him.)*
Deirdre And you take care.
Barry I won't go looking for trouble.
Deirdre To heck with trouble! I don't want you looking for other women! I'm still wondering who this Layla is.
Barry It's a... it's a ... a record by Derek and the Dominoes. It was on the radio earlier.
Deirdre Mm, so you say. Now, have you worked out a plan of action?
Barry I thought I'd start at the Manor.
Deirdre I'd help you, but Mum's waiting for this shopping. And tonight I've got to stay in and play Scrabble with Auntie Eileen.
Barry Isn't she the one who cheats?
Deirdre Yes, she puts any old letters down, and when we question the

The Scent of Danger

	word, she claims we're picking on her because she's old and losing her memory. It's easier to let her have her own way. You could join us if you wanted.
Barry	Thanks, but I may be still working.
Deirdre	But it'll be dark soon.
Barry	I've got a torch. And you can spot cats best at night. You can see their eyes glowing in the dark.
Deirdre	Just so long as it's only cats' eyes that are glowing! *(She puts on her scarf and coat as she speaks.)* You know, Barry, I'm having second thoughts about this occupation you've taken on. It might be exciting, but it could turn nasty. Perhaps you'd be better off with a proper job. You know, a nine-to-five, where you get to wear a smart suit, and get a regular income. When we're married, I don't want to be reading about you in the papers after they've dragged your frozen body from the canal, all dripping weed and water, your feet in concrete slippers, and your little body full of bullet holes…
Barry	Deirdre, you watch far too much late night television! You're scaring the pants off me!
Deirdre	*(giving him a hug)* I told you before - we'll have none of that till after the wedding! Now, go get 'em tiger! *(In a dreadful American accent.)* But hey! You be careful out there!
Barry	*(putting on his hat and pulling the brim down)* OK, you cat-nappers. Better run and hide, cos Hank Silver is a-coming after you!
Deirdre	I thought *you* were taking on this job?
Barry	*(ignoring her)* And anyone who gets in Hank's way is gonna know about it! *(Barry swaggers towards the door, and as he reaches it, it flies open and Luigi Salini comes in. He is a middle-aged Italian, swarthy and dark-haired. He wears a suit and gloves. He grabs Barry by the lapels. Barry struggles but cannot escape. He gasps for breath.)*
Luigi	Ah, Mr Bigley. I've been wanting a word with you. You're proving to be a very elusive tenant.
Deirdre	You leave him alone, you big bully! *(She swings her shopping at him. Luigi lets go. Barry slumps onto the bed, gasping for breath.)* Can't you see he has a weak chest?
Barry	*(weakly)* It's - it's all right. This is Mr Salini, my landlord.
Deirdre	He's got a very physical way of collecting rents.
Luigi	Who is this spitting cat?

Deirdre I don't spit - well, not since I had my teeth fixed. And I'm Barry's fiancée, and that means we're one, so if you molest him, you molest me!

Luigi It would have to be a very desperate man who would even consider molesting *you!*

Deirdre Did you hear that, Barry. Hit him!

Barry I think we ought to carefully consider the matter first.

Luigi All I am after is my legal entitlement. *(He moves C.)* According to our agreement, you were to pay me one month's rent in advance.

Barry Which is what I did.

Luigi But that was two months ago, and I have not seen another penny. And among my many gifts, I do not number patience as one of them.

Barry It's just that you haven't been around for me to give it to you.

Luigi I have been out of the country, but now I am back and I want my money.

Barry All right, Mr Salini. I'll get you your rent.

Luigi Good I do so hate unpleasantness.

Deirdre Tell me, Mr Saliva. If you're the landlord, why don't you control your other tenants, instead of bullying my Barry?

Luigi In what way?

Deirdre Those people downstairs have left their caravan right across the pavement. Barry wants to make an official complaint against them.

Barry I never said...

Luigi It happens to be my caravan. And your complaint is pointless as it's not there at the moment. And there are no tenants downstairs. Unfortunately, I have not found anyone to take over the flat, which is another reason I need the rent. I may yet have to live in the place myself.

Barry That'll be nice, won't it, Deirdre, having Mr Salini as a neighbour?

Deirdre Like having a boil on your bum!

Luigi I think you had better tell your mother here to keep her mouth shut, Mr Bigley.

Deirdre His mother?

Barry Yes, I think you had better keep out of this mum..., er, Deirdre. *(He stands.)* The thing is, Mr Salini, I don't have the money on me at the moment. *(Luigi makes a threatening move towards him.)* But I'm going down to the bank right now, and I'll bring

	you the money.
Luigi	Perhaps I ought to keep your lady friend here until you get back.
Deirdre	You do and I'll scream the place down. *(Puts her bags down and sits on the bed.)*
Barry	And believe me, she can certainly scream. I recall once when I tried to undo her blouse...
Luigi	Spare me the sordid details of your relationship, please. All right, I shall give you one more day. I shall return tomorrow, with a few friends of mine.
Deirdre	You've got friends? Yeah, tell us another!
Luigi	These friends are also very impatient people.
Barry	In that case, could I have a quick word with my fiancée? In private?
Luigi	If you must. I will wait on the landing. But do not take long. *(Exits.)*
Deirdre	What's the matter?
Barry	Have you any money?
Deirdre	Not much. I keep using up my wages to buy little things for my bottom drawer.
Barry	It's just that, when I said I'd go to the bank, I don't think there'd be much point.
Deirdre	Silly! Banks are the best place to draw out money.
Barry	Yes, but it helps if you've got a bank account to start with.
Deirdre	But you told me you were saving up for our wedding. And for our little cottage, and for the nursery, and everything.
Barry	I doubt I could afford to buy the cat flap at the moment, Deirdre. I'm broke. See that old typewriter over there? It should be a top of the range computer, only I can't even afford the mouse.
Deirdre	*(wailing)* Oh, Barry! How could you?
Barry	It's only a temporary setback. I used all my savings setting up this business. I did it for us, darling. You see, with an ordinary job, by the time we'd saved up the deposit on the cottage, and all that stuff to furnish it, well, we'd be going up the aisle on zimmer frames. But if this business takes off, we'll be coining it in, in no time. Think of what I'll be getting for this lost cat job, for instance.
Deirdre	*(somewhat mollified)* I suppose you're right. But he said you could have till tomorrow to pay.
Barry	Better to pay him now. I don't fancy meeting his 'friends'.

ACT I Scene 1

	They're probably the type who'd make an interesting TV documentary on Neanderthal Man.
Deirdre	We'll call the police.
Barry	And tell them what? If I pay him, he'll go away. I wish I'd asked that Suzanne for an advance. What am I going to do?
Deirdre	It's like those cowboy films. What we need is the cavalry to come charging up...
	(From the landing, we hear Ethel's voice.)
Ethel	*(off)* Aren't you the landlord of this building?
Luigi	*(off)* I have that honour, madam.
Ethel	*(off)* Then why don't you fit a lift? Why should us old ladies have to struggle up and down stairs in this day and age, eh? Answer me that?
Luigi	*(off)* Madam, will you stop poking me in the chest?
Barry	It's the cavalry, Deirdre! *(He hugs her, then crosses to door and opens it.)* What are you doing back here?
Ethel	*(entering, carrying the vacuum cleaner)* Have you forgotten already? It's Monday. I come to clean for you on Mondays.
Barry	But you've been once today.
Ethel	Nonsense! I'd have remembered something like that. Oh, am I disturbing you?
Deirdre	No, it's all right, Mrs Bigley. I was just going.
Barry	Honest, Mum, you were here not long ago.
Ethel	You're a rum lad, you know, our Barry. You're always teasing your old Mum. *(She holds up the plug.)* Now, where's your thingy?
Barry	But surely Dad must have mentioned you've been once?
Ethel	To tell the truth, he's that wrapped up in them quiz shows, he doesn't know what day it is half the time. *(She laughs.)* Do you know, he goes to the library and half an hour later, he's forgotten he's been. Now that's a sign of old age creeping up on you! I said, where's your thingy?
Barry	Just a minute, Mum. You might just be able to save my life.
Ethel	Oh, it's no good asking me to do that artificial perspiration, son, or that mouth to mouth stuff. I'm not that bothered about kissing your Dad, let alone complete strangers.
Barry	It's like this, I need money and I need it right away.
Ethel	I thought we already gave you your pocket money this week?
Barry	I need a bit more than pocket money. You see that man out on the landing?
Ethel	He's your landlord. I told him to get a lift put in.

The Scent of Danger

Barry I owe him rent and he's rather anxious to have it right away.
Ethel Tell him you'll pay your rent when he gets a lift put in and not before. It's the only way to get things done. He's only picking on you because you're weak and skinny. Ask him if he's using strong arm tic-tacs on the people in the flat downstairs.
Barry That's probably why they moved out.
Ethel Then use the Bigley charm on him.
Deirdre I don't think he's the amenable type, Mrs Bigley.
Ethel Armenian, is he? He looks foreign.
Barry Mum? Money?
Ethel I don't have any on me, son, sorry.
Barry That's it, then. I'm dead.
Ethel You look all right from here. A bit peaky, but what do you expect with a face like yours? Anyway, can't stand here chatting, I've got work to do. Did you tell me where your thingy was?
Deirdre What are we going to do?
Barry Search me. We need some more cavalry, but ones who've been paid.
Luigi *(enters from the landing.)* All right, you have had enough time. *(He moves C. From the landing we hear Sidney's voice.)*
Sidney *(off)* Ethel? Are you up here?
Ethel In here, Sid. I just popped in to do Barry's flat.
Sidney *(entering)* You great daft bat! You've been here once today! Honest, Barry, I don't know what's up with her, but she'll be forgetting her name next. I parked up so we could do a bit of late-night shopping and by the time I'd bought an evening paper, she'd disappeared.
Barry How did you guess she'd come back here?
Sidney Because the hoover had disappeared with her. Come on, woman! Home!
Barry Before you go, Dad, could you do me a big favour?
Sidney I'm already doing you a big favour by taking your mother off your hands.
Barry No, something more than that.
Sidney You want me to take Deirdre too? No problem, son. You'll work better with no women around.
Barry Do you have any cash with you? That I could borrow?
Sidney *(shaking his head)* I don't carry cash around with me. Not with all these muggers about.

ACT I Scene 1

Ethel	He's telling fibs, Barry. He never lets that redundancy money out of his sight. Doesn't trust banks, so he carries it round with him in one of them money belts under his shirt.
Sidney	Shut up, woman! There's a total stranger in the room.
Luigi	Do not worry. I only want my rights.
Ethel	Loan him some money, Sid.
Sidney	Do I have to?
Deirdre	He is your son, Mr Bigley.
Sidney	That's why I'd rather not. If he's family, he might not pay it back.
Barry	I will, Dad, honest. First opportunity I have.
Sidney	Oh well, if I must. *(He starts to unbuckle his trouser belt then looks at Luigi.)* I'm not showing him what I've got.
Luigi	I can assure you I am not in the slightest bit interested in what you have got.
Sidney	Even so, there are women present.
Barry	Come into the bathroom.
	(Barry and Sidney exit DR.)
Ethel	Nice weather for the time of year.
Luigi	I hadn't noticed. I have just come back from a country where the sun always shines.
Ethel	I could tell you've been abroad, you with your tan and all. So, are you going to install it?
Luigi	Install what?
Ethel	The lift. Now you're getting your money, you can put in a lift.
Luigi	I have no intention of wasting money on such luxuries. I have bigger fish to fry.
Ethel	You're setting up a chip shop? That's a good idea. Do you know chip shops are vanishing off our streets? I blame it on all this foreign food. All you see in the High Street now is them pizzas and pastas, or whatever they're called. Foreign muck, I call it!
Deirdre	Mrs Bigley, I don't think…
Ethel	But if you're frying fish, we'll be your first customers.
	(Enter Barry and Sidney from DR. Barry hands over the money to Luigi.)
Luigi	Just make sure you are on time next month. *(Exits, laughing.)*
Ethel	Well, I never! Not even a please or thank you, or a kiss my ar…
Barry	Mum!

The Scent of Danger

Ethel I was going to say 'arm'. I hope we don't see *him* again. And I'm definitely not buying his fish and chips now!
Barry Thanks, Dad. You don't know how much that meant to me.
Sidney I know exactly how much it meant to *me*, son!
Barry I'll pay you back as soon as I can. In fact, I'm on a big case now which should have stacks of money in it.
Ethel If you've got a big case full of stacks of money, why are you borrowing from your Dad?
Sidney She gets dafter! Anyway, son, now you're set up, there's a little favour you can do for me.
Barry Anything at all.
Sidney I'd rather discuss it on a person to person basis.
Deirdre *(standing)* Don't worry about me. I've got to get home before my frozen melts.
Ethel Frozen what, love? You look warm enough to me in that coat.
Barry And I really should be searching for a cat.
Ethel I can help you there. If you want a cat, go to Pullins Pet Shop. They have some lovely tabbies in the window.
Barry Thanks for that, Mum.
Ethel Any time, son. I'd do anything to make you happy. I've already bought my hat, you know - for the wedding. So when you decide to say the word... *(Starts to sob.)*
Sidney What's up with you now?
Ethel Ooh, I *love* weddings. It's only time I can have a good cry without Sid saying 'What's up with you now?'
Deirdre Give us a kiss.
Ethel Oh, all right then. *(Kisses Deirdre on the cheek.)*
Deirdre I meant... oh, what the heck. *(She kisses Barry then picks up her bags.)* Oh damn! My runner beans are running! *(Exits to landing.)*
Sidney Thank you, then, Ethel.
Ethel I haven't given you anything, have I?
Sidney No, I meant, would you mind making yourself scarce while I have a word with Barry?
Ethel Oh, I understand. Yes, it's about time he knew, what with him courting Deirdre.
Barry Knew what?
Ethel I don't like to say it in front of your father, but do the words 'gooseberry bush' mean anything to you?
Barry You've got some in your garden.

ACT I Scene 1

Ethel Precisely. But bear in mind, that's where they should stay. After all, we don't want you and Deirdre having unwanted little gooseberries running about the place, do we?
Barry I quite like gooseberries.
Ethel And that's the root of the trouble, Barry. You understand what I'm talking about, don't you?
Barry Frankly, Mum, I haven't the faintest.
Ethel That's all right, because your father will give you the details. I'll leave you two to talk man's talk. I'll just pop in and clean the bathroom. *(Exits DR.)*
Barry Have you any idea what that was about?
Sidney Haven't the foggiest, son, but then your mother's mind would baffle a bevy of psychiatrists.
Barry What was it you were wanting to talk to me about?
Sidney It's something I'm working on to give me a fighting chance in one of the quizzes.
Barry Which one?
Sidney I thought of applying for 'Countdown'.
Barry You need a good grasp of the language for that.
Sidney I'm more worried about the time limit and the tension - you know, that great clock ticking away and that music - enough to frighten anyone.
Barry So how do you plan to tackle it?
Sidney I've been knocking some things up in the shed, some props to help me train. Only your mother has refused point blank to let me set them up in the house. She claims it makes the place look untidy.
Barry So, how can I help?
Sidney I was wondering if you'd look after them for me? They don't take up much room, and when I'm in town, I can pop in and have a practise.
Barry I am trying to run a business here, Dad.
Sidney I appreciate that, son, but you're my only hope. And I need hardly remind you that I've just saved your bacon vis-á-vis that landlord of yours.
Barry Point taken. Bring the stuff up when you like. I suppose it'll only be temporary?
Sidney When I get on the real thing, I can chuck it all away.
Barry When would you like to bring it? Tomorrow OK?
Sidney It just so happens that I've got it outside. Ethel gave it its marching orders this very afternoon. It's all right. You'll hardly

The Scent of Danger

notice it's here. Virtually invisible, it is. Thanks, Barry.
Barry   Do you want a hand?
Sidney   Appreciate it, son.
(Barry and Sidney exit onto landing and Sidney returns carrying a cardboard box which he dumps on floor at foot of bed, then he goes to help Barry, who enters with a cardboard clock as big as himself. They have great difficulty fitting it through the door. They prop it on the bed.)
Barry   Virtually invisible, you said!
Sidney   You'll hardly notice it -when the light's out.
Barry   Does it work?
Sidney   Don't be daft! It's cardboard! You see, it's all psychological. They try to make you feel small by having this massive clock hanging over you. I can practise with this and get used to it being around. Then, when I go on the show, I won't feel oppressed.
Barry   *I* will, having that great thing hovering over my bed.
Sidney   It's all for the good of the family, son.
Barry   Even so, what are my clients going to say? They'll think I'm timing their every move. And what's in that box?
Sidney   That's full of the cards marked with consonants and vowels.
Ethel   *(enters from DR.)* You're supposed to be teaching him the facts of life, Sid, not talking about your toilet habits.
Sidney   I said *vowels,* Ethel.
Ethel   I know. I heard.
Sidney   A, E, I, O, U.
Ethel   Are you in pain, Sid? Are you getting them stones in your gizzard again?
Sidney   The only stones around here are in your head, Ethel!
Ethel   I see your father's brought you a nice present for your office, Barry. He did try to put it in our front room, but I said it wasn't as nice as that little carriage clock your Uncle Sandy gave us for an anniversary present. Pity it's missing a hand - *that* clock, not the carriage clock your Uncle Sandy bought us. Still you'll be able to tell the time right across the office.
Barry   You'd be able to tell the time right across town!
Sidney   So we'll be going, lad. Thanks again for you know…
Barry   Thanks for the loan.
Sidney   And I'll be popping in soon to practise, OK?
Barry   Any time you like.

Ethel	Weren't you looking for a cat?
Barry	Lord yes! I was hoping to have tracked it down by now.
Ethel	You're going to be disappointed. Pullins will have shut.
Barry	I've got an alternative source.
Ethel	Have you? We'll try it next time you come for dinner. Can't get your Dad to eat anything but HP.
Sidney	We'll be off, then.
Ethel	I hope the flat's clean enough for you, Barry.
Barry	It's so clean, you could eat off the floor.
Ethel	Remind me to buy him some plates, Sid. You'd think, for the rent he gets, these flats would come with all mod cons.

(Ethel and Sidney exit onto landing.)

Barry Thank goodness for that. *(In an American accent.)* Hank tipped his hat to the back of his head and reflected on his narrow escape. The Mafia had sent their top man, but they'd not reckoned with Hank's quick wit and lion-like courage. It would take someone bigger and better than Three-Fingers Flattery to put the frighteners on a private eye with Hank's experience. With that little spot of bother out of the way, it was time for Layla. Hank's heart beat faster as he recalled the way she had filled the office with her presence, how her slim frame had occupied that chair, her smile lighting up the room and warming his very soul. Now he knew he had to come through for her, to prove himself to her, to show her he was unafraid, unashamed - a real man! He squared his shoulders and set off - *(Normal voice.)* to find her bloomin'' cat!

(He switches off the lights, then exits to landing, closing and locking the door. Landing light fades to indicate the passing of time.)

ACT I Scene 2

Same scene, around one hour later. Landing light fades up. There is a slight pause, then a shadow appears on the glass of the door. Someone inserts a key and the door opens to reveal Luigi. He carries a gun. He looks around, then moves cautiously across the room and exits to bathroom DR. He comes back and goes back to the landing door.

Luigi Bring her in - quickly! *(A figure, dressed all in black and with his face obscured by a balaclava helmet with eyeholes, enters, pulling Suzanne in with him. She has her hands bound and is*

The Scent of Danger 37

gagged. She struggles, but they force her into the desk chair.) Keep still, my pretty pizza. *(Luigi switches on the desk light.)* We will not detain you long, just long enough to get your father to produce the ransom money. It won't cost him much, just the equivalent of a couple of his diamonds. But a fortune to me. *(He puts paper in typewriter and types as he talks.)* Right, what shall we say? Your daughter is alive, but her safe return will cost you... what shall we say, young lady? Two hundred thousand pounds? Better make it a round quarter of a million. Phone this number tonight for details. And no police, if you want your daughter to keep her good looks. There we are. Good job I watch your excellent police TV series. *(To other man.)* I want you to take her to the flat below. There's no furniture, but lock her in one of the built-in cupboards. Then take this *(He hands over the paper.)* and deliver it to the Manor by hand - without being seen. *(To Suzanne.)* Smooth, don't you agree? But the caravan, that was a stroke of genius. So typically English to see one parked up in a town centre car park, and so convenient for Hattie's Salon too. OK take her downstairs.

(Luigi switches off the desk light and they hustle Suzanne out of the office. Luigi closes and locks the door. Landing light fades to indicate the passing of time.)

ACT I Scene 3

Same scene. It is around midnight. The office is in darkness, but the light on the landing is on. The phone rings. After a couple of rings, the answer phone clicks on. We hear Barry's recorded American voice.

Barry (recorded) Hi. I'm not around at the moment, but if you want to give me hard cash, then leave it in unmarked notes at the Tax Office. He'd only get it anyway, so cut out the middleman. If you want to leave a message, speak after the tone. Chow.

Voice *(upper class, on phone)* You've got the upper hand at the moment, you scum, so I'll go along with this disgraceful business. But you lay one finger on my daughter, and, by God, I'll hunt you down!

(The phone is slammed down. There is a pause of a few seconds, then Barry unlocks the landing door. He enters, switches on the bedside lamp, then, yawning, moves C. He takes off his hat, throws it at the hat rack and misses, and the hat goes out through the window.)

Barry Damn! *(He stretches his aching back, then goes to the desk switches on desk light and sits down, picks up a pen and*

ACT I Scene 3

opens a notebook.) Let's see, then. The Case of Cleopatra - progress report one. Went to the Manor. Didn't reach the house as they keep a Rottweiler - a fact dear Suzanne didn't bother to mention. Decided to have a look round from the upper branches of a nearby tree, but no sign of the cat. When dog got bored, searched lane leading towards the Manor. Widened search to take in fields either side of lane. *(To himself.)* She also forgot to mention the herds of cows. Took me ages to scrape that stuff off my shoes. *(Writing.)* Explained to angry farmer with shotgun that I was not trying to rustle his cattle. Went back to entrance to Manor and saw black car coming out of drive. Maybe Cleopatra has been cat-napped. *(To himself.)* And why not? Rich family, pampered pet - and that's only Suzanne! Nah! This is England. Things like that don't happen here. *(Writing.)* Ended search 11.30pm. Will resume at first light. *(He puts down his pen, yawns again and turns towards the bed, jumping when he sees the clock.)* I forgot that thing was there. *(He moves C, adopting the American accent.)* Hank suddenly knew the meaning of loneliness. The room, though empty, still retained a subtle hint of Layla's perfume. But all he was left with was the ghost of her presence. *(There is a faint, far-off tapping noise. Barry stands and listens. In his normal voice.)* Ghosts? Come on, Barry, you're tired, that's all. A good night's sleep and...*(There is a single, loud thump. Barry rushes to the landing door and pulls it open.)* Hello? Is there anyone out there? *(He comes back into the room, closing the door behind him. He takes off his coat and hangs it up, throws his jacket on the bed and unbuckles his belt. The tapping starts again.)* Rick? Is that you messing about? *(Loud thump.)* Oh God! Maybe those notes Dad gave me were forged! Mr ... Mr Salini? Is that you? Well, I'm calling the police, you hear? You can't frighten me. *(He stands in the middle of the room and adopts a karate stance.)* I'm ready for you, Salini! *(His trousers fall round his ankles. He grabs them and hoists them up again as we see a tall, angular shadow on the glass of the landing door.)* What the hell's that? Are the Mafia using robots now? *(There is a loud thump. The door slowly starts to open. He grabs the counterpane off the bed and hurls it over the intruder as they enter. It is, in fact, Ethel, carrying her hoover in front of her. She cries out.)*

Ethel Help! Muggers! Vandals! Teddy Boys!
Barry *(freeing her)* It's me, mum.
Ethel Help! I'm being mugged by my own son!

The Scent of Danger

Barry	Sorry, Mum. But how was I to know it was you? What are you doing here at this time of night?
Ethel	I just couldn't sleep, son. It's your Dad. He talks all night long, asking himself questions and answering them -yakkity yak, yakkity yak! So I thought as I was wide awake, I'd pop over and give you a clean-up. *(She holds up the hoover plug.)* Er, where's your thingy?
Barry	*(collapses into his desk chair and looks at the ceiling.)* Why me? Why me?

(As the lights fade, we hear a thumping noise, muffled but getting louder. Then it stops and the Curtain falls.)

ACT II

Same scene. It is early morning the next day and the sun is just starting to shine through the window. Barry is in bed in pyjamas. The clock is leaning against the landing door. There is a loud knocking on the door.

Barry	Wha...? Wha's that?
Rick	*(off)* Barry! Open up. It's me, Rick!
Barry	It's not locked.
	(The door flies open, the clock falls over and Rick sprawls in on top of the clock.)
Rick	What the...? *(Picking himself up.)* I've seen some burglar alarms in my time, but this has to be the daftest!
Barry	Sorry. It's a long story.
Rick	Then you'll be able to time it won't you? Why are you still in bed?
Barry	I'm tired, OK? I was up till all hours searching for that cat. When I got back, someone in the block was hammering away. I thought there were laws against people doing DIY that time of night. And I never found that damn cat!
Rick	Never mind Cleopatra. There's a much bigger case for you to take on.
Barry	*(sitting up)* Someone lost their hamster, have they?
Rick	Will you listen? Suzanne's gone!
Barry	Took off, did she? Well, you can hardly blame her, can you? I never understood what she saw in you in the first place.
Rick	Pay attention! She's missing!

ACT II

Barry (*yawning*) Missing what? She seemed to have all the requisite - and exquisite - bits last time I saw her.
Rick Will you stop rambling and concentrate?
Barry Just a minute. What time is it?
Rick A little after eight.
Barry That's the middle of the night.
Rick You've got to get up! Suzanne's been kidnapped!
Barry Kidnapped! (*He laughs.*) Yeah, good one, Rick. Still doing the practical jokes, are we? I remember when you spread chilli on my school dinner sarnies instead of chutney. For the rest of the day, every time I burped, I set fire to my books.
Rick Stop ranting and listen! At the risk of sounding like a B-movie script, this is a matter of life and death. And will you get up? (*Goes to pull the covers off Barry.*)
Barry OK, I'm up. (*He gets out of bed.*) You'd better tell me the whole story.
Rick That's what I'm trying to do.
Barry You talk - I'll get washed. (*Takes his clothes and exits to bathroom DR.*)
Rick (*pacing round the clock*) Why *do* you have a cardboard clock in your flat? Latest in floor coverings, is it?
Barry (*off*) Take too long to explain.
Rick Well, I went to the Manor to pick up Suzanne this morning. She had a modelling session in York and she had an early start. Anyway, I arrives at the house to find her father nearly off his head with rage. I thought he was going to drag me out of the cab and throttle me on the spot for just daring to exist. He's a pretty big bloke at the best of times, and this morning he seems to have grown another two feet.
Barry (*off*) Means he could chase you off his property twice as fast.
Rick What does?
Barry (*off*) Having four feet!
Rick This is no time for jokes, believe me. He scared the living daylights out of me. Apparently, it was all my fault. I was supposed to meet her last night after she had been to Hattie's for her massage. Only she always takes ages when she goes there, so I went down the pub. And guess who was in there! Harry! You remember Harry Lansdown from school? Used to be a prefect - always giving you lines.
Barry (*off*) For crimes *you* had usually committed.
Rick Yes, well you could never run as fast as me. Anyway, I haven't

The Scent of Danger

seen him for years. Did you know he's running a bookies in Brum?

Barry (*off*) Now who's wasting time?

Rick Sorry. We had a few bevvies and a chat about the old days, and then Harry invited me back to his hotel and we carried on drinking. The fact that I was supposed to meet Suze went clean out of my head.

Barry (*enters from DR, dressed and combing his hair.*) Oh, sure. Suzanne is just the sort you can easily forget!

Rick Well, I'd had a fair few to drink by that time. Anyway, she was in her own car last night, and I certainly wasn't fit to drive. I finally flaked out at home in the early hours. At least I remembered I had to take her to York this morning.

Barry Big of you. If I had a lovely lass like Suzanne as my girlfriend, I wouldn't forget she even existed for one minute.

Rick I'm sorry, OK? I didn't mean to offend your chivalrous nature.

Barry (*sitting on the bed to put on his socks and shoes*) So, what did her father say?

Rick I eventually persuaded him not to organise a lynching party and he told me she didn't come home last night. By midnight, he was starting to get worried, so he went to have a look out the front door, and there was this note lying on the mat.

Barry What, ten pound note or something?

Rick Do you think of anything else but money?

Barry Not when I haven't any.

Rick It was a ransom note.

Barry What did it say? Have you got it with you?

Rick He didn't give it me.

Barry Pity. Did you get a look at it?

Rick A quick glance, that's all.

Barry Was it made up of letters cut from newspapers?

Rick You watch too many movies! It was just a typed note.

Barry Typed or printed?

Rick How do I know? It was just black letters.

Barry (*moving to desk*) Pity you couldn't have pinched it. You see, typewriters like this clapped-out heap are all different, and by comparing typefaces, you can narrow it down to one machine.

Rick So you intend to contact every office in town and ask for a sample from their typewriters? Suzanne would be drawing her pension before you'd got through them all.

Barry The problem is, hardly anyone uses typewriters nowadays,

ACT II

and I'm not sure if the same typeface differences apply to computer printers.

Rick He gave me the gist of the note. Seemed the usual sort of thing - you know, if you want your daughter back, hand over a quarter of a million in used notes. And if he contacted the police, Suzanne would never be able to face the cameras again.

Barry She'd be too scared, you mean?

Rick Too *scarred*, you idiot!

Barry Oh, my God! We can't allow that! That face is perfection!

Rick There was one thing in the note. It gave a phone number which he had to ring for further instructions.

Barry That's a clue. A phone number can be traced.

Rick The police might be able to demand that sort of information, but I doubt you can.

Barry It might be in the phone book.

Rick So it might. And at this moment, the entire servant population of Snaresby Manor is checking every number in a very thick book. But it might not be in if it's ex-directory or has only recently been installed.

Barry But he must have got some information from calling the number.

Rick It was an answering machine and it just told him where to leave the money.

Barry *(eagerly)* Now we're getting somewhere! Where was he to leave it?

Rick Don't ask me. He wasn't going to divulge the location of two hundred and fifty thousand smackers to a mere mini-cab driver, was he? Anyway, when I mentioned you, he said at least you weren't the law, so you might be able to do something. So long as you don't go blabbing it all over town.

Barry Do you honestly think I'd risk anything happening to that face? To that gorgeous, lovely, beauti…

Rick For crying out loud! Will you get away from this fixation with her features? This is all Deirdre's fault, you know.

Barry Where does she come into it?

Rick If you'd had a halfway decent-looking girlfriend in the first place, you wouldn't have gone ga-ga when you clapped your lecherous eyes on a looker like Suzanne.

Barry Has her father delivered the money yet?

Rick Not yet. He's holding out as long as he can.

The Scent of Danger

Barry You said she had her car last night. Any sign of that?
Rick Vanished off the face of the earth.
Barry So, what's the plan?
Rick Isn't that your job? You're the private eye, aren't you?
Barry Of course I am! *(Dejectedly.)* I don't know, Rick. Perhaps he'd be better employing a professional.
Rick What is up with you? You *are* a professional!
Barry Maybe for the odd missing cat, or a lost wallet, but this is big time. Someone could get hurt.
Rick Er, her father did say something about one per cent of the ransom…
Barry One per cent? Why, that's… that's… that's a hell of a lot of bread!
Rick Loaves and loaves of it.
Barry You're right, Rick. Someone in desperate trouble needs my skills, and she's going to get them. Right! What's the plan?
Rick You mean you *still* haven't worked out a plan?
Barry Give me a chance. I have to assimilate the facts.
Rick I bet Hank Silver would have worked out a plan by now.
Barry What do you know about Hank Silver?
Rick If I recall aright, he was your hero at Saturday morning pictures. Fictional American private eye, wasn't he? Always solved crimes in minutes flat and always got the gorgeous girl too. You used to talk in that terrible fake Yankee accent. 'Course that was years ago, when you were a youngster. I'm sure you left all that rubbish behind when you grew up.
Barry *(clearing his throat)* Er, naturally I did. Here, give me a hand with this, will you?
(Barry and Rick prop the clock on the bed.)
Rick Tell me, is this for some weird sexual game you and Deirdre play? Sort of 'beat the clock' or something?
Barry I'm surprised you mention the words 'sex' and 'Deirdre' in the same sentence.
Rick Still saving herself for marriage is she? You lucky feller! OK - the plan?
Barry Er, yes, the plan. *(He strides round the office muttering to himself.)* It'd be best if we… no, that's no good. Perhaps we should… no, that's useless…
Rick How about getting all the active bods out on the street? There are some empty offices on the far side of town, or those old garages in Church Street. We should at least search those

	first. We might find her car and that'd be a start.
Barry	Good idea! We could split the town into sections.
Rick	Who else can you get to search?
Barry	Well there's you, and there's me... Then there's you... and then there's me...
Rick	What about Deirdre? She's got a good nose on her.
Barry	Do you have to keep insulting her all the time?
Rick	I meant, for ferreting things out.
Barry	She might be somewhat loath to help Suzanne. But if I tell her what the money would buy, I think she'll join us. It's her day off, so I'll call round.
Rick	Good, that's settled then. What about the office?
Barry	What about the office?
Rick	Someone'll have to hang about here, so we have a central base to report in to.
Barry	Exactly what I was thinking.
Rick	Well then?
Barry	Well what?
Rick	Who's going to man the office?
Barry	I suppose I could do it...
Rick	Except you're needed out on the street.
Barry	I can't think of anyone.
Rick	We need someone who won't ask too many questions. The less people know the truth, the better for Suzanne's safety. We need someone who'll happily sit around in here without wanting to know the reason why.
Barry	Oh, come on, Rick! Who'd be daft enough to do something without any reason whatsoever?
	(Ethel arrives on the landing with her hoover. She is panting.)
Ethel	Are you up yet, Barry, love? I've come to clean.
Rick	The answer to our prayers!
Ethel	Ooh, I'm not disturbing you boys at morning prayer, am I?
Rick	Just finished, Mrs B. I'll leave it to you then, Barry, while I get moving.
Barry	Phone straight away if you've any news. Here's the number.
	(He takes a card from the desk and hands it to Rick.)
Rick	Bye then, Mrs Bigley.
Ethel	Oh, are you going? I hope it wasn't something I said. And I haven't got BO, not since I started using that soap that actress swears by. Mind, Mr Bigley say there's too much swearing on

The Scent of Danger

television. He says, when he gets famous, he's going to make everyone on the tele' speak proper - like what he does.

Rick It's nothing you've said, Mrs B. I've just got things to do.

Ethel Here, I know you, don't I? Didn't you used to go to school with my Barry? Let me see... it's Dick, no, Mick, no, Nick... it rhymes with 'sick' anyway. I remember that because you were always sick on the coach when we went on a chara trip. I've never seen anything like it. It used to flood out, all over...

Barry Thank you, Mum. You can spare us the details.

Rick Tell you what. We'll cover a bigger area if I take the cab and cruise round a bit.

Barry Good idea.

Rick I'm on my way.

Ethel Right, Barry. Where's your thingy? *(Hangs her coat and scarf on the stand.)*

Barry Usual place.

Ethel Have you only just got up? You've left that bed in a right mess.

Barry I had a disturbed night. The bloke downstairs was hammering away till Lord knows what hour, building shelves, or something.

Ethel *(tidying the bed)* Your landlord told me there was no one living down there.

Barry In that case, there are some very noisy ghosts in the building. Leave the bed, Mum, I'll do it later.

Ethel You see, you're not like your Dad. He was in the army, National Service. In the Army, you're not allowed to make a mess of your bed, in case you're inspected at a moment's notice. So he learned to lie to attention all night long. Takes a lot of discipline to do that, son, lie still without moving a muscle. He got so good at it, he couldn't get out of the habit when he was demobbed. It did have its drawbacks, though. It made it devilish difficult when we were trying for you.

Barry Look, I have to go out and I need you to do me a favour.

Ethel Anything at all, Barry, so long as it doesn't involve a great deal of thinking. Your Dad says that at my age, I have to rest my brain in case it wears out too quickly.

Barry This will take no brain work at all. I just need someone to sit in here, answer the phone if it rings, and pass on any messages that might come through.

Ethel Does this involve writing?

Barry It might.

ACT II

Ethel	I never got to grips with these ballpoint pens. It was on account of them terrible pens they gave you when I was at school. The nibs used to get twisted, and the ink was so runny, what I put down came out more like 'wronging' than 'writing'.
Barry	Use a pencil.
Ethel	My teacher used to say my writing looked like spider had crawled into the inkwell and then staggered drunkenly across the paper. But it shows the value of education, Barry. Until that moment, I was totally unaware that spiders drank alcohol. Still, it explains why they have the nerve to hang upside down from ceilings.
Barry	So you'll do it? Look after the office?
Ethel	For you, son, of course. I'll see that no one pinches it while you're away.
Barry	Thanks. I suppose that's the best I can expect.
Ethel	Can I get someone to help me?
Barry	You mean Dad?
Ethel	No, he's down the bookshop looking for quiz questions. I was thinking of our next door neighbour - you know, Gladys. She usually comes in for a cup of tea of a morning. Maybe we can have it here instead.
Barry	Whatever you think best, Mum. Give her a ring. I'll see you later. (*He goes to the door and pauses, waiting to see what Ethel does. Ethel sits at the desk and gingerly picks up the phone.*)
Ethel	Hello? Operator? Can I speak to Gladys please?
Barry	I'll do it shall I? (*Crosses and takes the phone.*)
Ethel	It's them new-fangled buttons. They confuse me.
Barry	What's her number?
Ethel	I've got it written on my hoover here. (*She reads.*) 50431... (*Barry starts to dial, repeating the numbers as Ethel calls them out.*)
Barry	Five, oh, four, three, one...
Ethel	...7, 5, 9, 8, 3...
Barry	Seven, five, nine, eight, three... Where's she live? Russia? (*He goes to look at the hoover.*) That's the serial number of the cleaner! Here's what you wrote. (*He dials.*) Six, three, three, five, one. It's ringing. Hello? Mrs Templeton? It's Barry Bigley - from next door... No, I'm not next door right at this moment... No, I can't pop in for a cup of tea right now... I'm phoning on behalf of my mother...No, she's not next door

The Scent of Danger

either... Mrs Cardoza, I am aware that my mother has lived next door to you for forty years, but that doesn't mean to say she's a permanent fixture... No, she hasn't flitted... Mum, you speak to her. Tell her you're near the centre of town, Flat 2 Brinsley Mansions. *(He hands her the phone.)* I must get moving. *(Exits to landing.)*

Ethel Hello? Gladys? Ooh, it's just like you're standing next to me... No, I can't come for a cuppa at the moment, I'm on the phone. No, you come to me today. Flat 2, Brinsley Mansions... No I haven't flitted without telling you. It's our Barry's flat - well, office really... No, I'm not at the Post Office! Can you come over right away? And bring the cards... Yes, Flat 2, Brinsons Mansley... That's it. See you soon. *(She holds the receiver at arms length before gingerly replacing it. She looks closely at the answer machine.)* I wonder if Barry knows his phone flashes? *(Presses buttons, then jumps back as Barry's message comes over.)*

Barry *(on answering machine)* Hi. I'm not around at the moment, but if you want to give me hard cash then leave it in used notes at the Tax Office. Well, they'll only get it anyway, so cut out the middle man. If you just want to leave a message, then speak after the tone. Chow.

Ethel *(looking around)* Barry? Where are you hiding? Come on, now. Don't play tricks on your old Mum. I know you're still here. I just heard your voice. *(Presses another button.)*

VOICE *(on answer machine)* You've got the upper hand at the moment, you scum, so I'll go along with this disgraceful business. But you lay one finger on my daughter and by God, I'll hunt you down!

(Ethel looks around for the source of the voice. She has her back to the landing door as Luigi appears in the open doorway. Ethel turns, sees him, and jumps.)

Ethel Ooh, my heart's all of a flutter! I don't like people creeping up on me.
Luigi I'm sorry, Mrs Bigley. The last thing I want to do is upset you.
Ethel You're the landlord, aren't you?
Luigi I have that honour.
Ethel You have the rent as well.
Luigi I know I have. I am here on another matter. Is your son in?
Ethel No, he's out.
Luigi Your husband?
Ethel He's not here either.

Luigi	Than you are here all alone?
Ethel	*(suspiciously)* Here, what do you want me on my own for? You're not after my honour, are you?
Luigi	Heaven forbid!
Ethel	A woman on her own isn't safe these days, not when she's kept her looks like I have. *(She fluffs her hair.)* And I've heard all about you Latin types. You're supposed to be very hot-blooded, aren't you?
Luigi	I assure you, madam, I am definitely not interested in your honour.
Ethel	You're sure?
Luigi	Positive.
Ethel	Pity. I get no fun these days. It's a good job I've got things to clean to keep me busy.
Luigi	I was wondering if your son had any phone calls last night.
Ethel	If he had, it's no concern of yours.
Luigi	It's just that we're having problems with the phone lines coming into this building.
Ethel	You'll have to ask Barry then, won't you?
Luigi	Have you taken any calls today?
Ethel	Here, what is this? The three degrees?
Luigi	Only enquiring. Also, have you heard any strange noises from the flat below?
Ethel	We have that! Leastwise my Barry has - a thumping noise. It kept him awake.
Luigi	You can tell him that I shall find out what was making the noise. It was probably the water in the pipes.
Ethel	You haven't put in that lift like I asked, have you?
Luigi	Mrs Bigley, it is not a job you can do in a moment. And I will need some help.
Ethel	It's no good looking at me! I haven't the strength to lift anything, let alone put lifts in.
Luigi	I meant help in the planning of it.
Ethel	I might. What have I got to do?
Luigi	Just go downstairs into the hall and have a look where you think the best place would be to install it.
Ethel	And you'd take my advice?
Luigi	Naturally. After all, you will be using it a lot, so if it's right for you, it will be right for everyone.
Ethel	Even my friend, Gladys? She's's very particular when it comes

The Scent of Danger

	to transport. She likes everything spotless - just like me. She always takes a little brush when she goes on a bus so she can dust the seat off.
Luigi	Whereas you take your vacuum cleaner.
Ethel	No, but it's not a bad idea, the state of bus seats these days.
Luigi	If you designed the lift, I'm sure that your friend will find it just right.
Ethel	Course she'd find it all right! She knows what a lift looks like! I'll just pop down and take a look. Oh, I forgot, I'm supposed to be looking after the office.
Luigi	It will be my pleasure to look after it in your absence, Mrs Bigley.
Ethel	I don't know... Barry was very pacific...
Luigi	But you both know me, don't you? It's not as if I'm a complete stranger.
Ethel	All right then. But I've counted the toilet rolls and tea bags.
Luigi	I shall touch nothing.
Ethel	Shan't be long.

(Ethel exits to landing. As soon as she is gone, Luigi rushes over to the desk.)

Luigi	I must be losing my touch. Fancy putting this idiot's telephone number on the note instead of the one downstairs! I'll have to find a way of getting the right one to him. Now, any messages? *(Pushes buttons on the answer machine.)*
VOICE	*(on machine)* You've got the upper hand at the moment, you scum, so I'll go along with this disgraceful business. But you lay a finger on my daughter and by God, I'll hunt you down!
Luigi	In your pretty pink jacket, no doubt! I'd better delete that. *(He presses buttons on the answer machine.)* Anyway, Mr Private Eye, should someone brighter than you trace the note or number, it will lead straight to you! Try explaining where you have hidden her.

(Ethel comes puffing into the office.)

Luigi	You have made a choice?
Ethel	Just a minute - let me get my breath. What you need is a lift up here.
Luigi	I thought that was what you were investigating.
Ethel	So I was! It'll have to go smack in the middle.
Luigi	You want the lift to make some sort of noise halfway up?
Ethel	No! Smack in the middle of the hallway. The front door of number one'll have to go.

ACT II

Luigi You wish me to destroy the front of one of my flats?
Ethel Just make it a bit, sort of, flatter, that's all. In fact, as no one's in there at the moment, you could start right away.
Luigi Much as I would like to, there are many considerations to be taken into account, such as planning permission and finance.
Ethel I knew it! By the time you get a lift, I'll be too old to use it.
Luigi I'm sure one day you will derive the benefit. Now, I really must get on. Thank you for your valuable assistance.
Ethel It was nothing.
Luigi It was rather more than you think! *(Exits to landing.)*
Ethel Now, where was I? He's thrown all my plans out - not that I had much of a plan...
(Gladys knocks on the door. She is Ethel's age, and wears flowing robes. She is very 'theatrical' in gesture and mannerisms. She is already slightly tipsy.)
Gladys You know Ethel, what is required here is a lift.
Ethel I've just been saying as much to the landlord.
Gladys Was he the gentleman I just passed on the stairs?
Ethel Aye, he's foreign.
Gladys I knew he must be. No Englishman would risk bad luck by passing one on the stairs.
Ethel Come in and make yourself at home.
Gladys *(moving C)* He's got a nice place here, has your boy.
Ethel I keep it spick and span for him.
Gladys You shouldn't be doing that, Ethel. You spoil him. You know the saying - spare the rod... You only have to look around to see what this free and easy upbringing has done to the youth of today.
Ethel But my Barry's a good lad.
Gladys Then why was he so anxious to move out into his own flat eh? I'll tell you. It's because they all want to live a life of *debauchery*! *(She says the last word with relish.)*
Ethel I'm not sure what that is, Gladys.
Gladys You know...*(She mouths the words.)* Free love!
Ethel Oh dear. I've heard about what went on at Bloodstock back in the sixties.
Gladys You want to keep a close eye on his antics, Ethel.
Ethel I don't think his Deirdre is the free love type.
Gladys They're all that type underneath, believe me. Just think on, that's all. *(She walks around taking deep breaths.)* Yes , there

The Scent of Danger

is a definite aura about this place.

Ethel I'll pop out and get a floral spray.

Gladys Not that sort of aura. I feel a definite presence.

Ethel That's because I'm standing right next to you, Gladys.

Gladys I'm glad you invited me over, Ethel. This is certainly a building which needs investigating. Tell me, has anyone died here?

Ethel I'm sure I wouldn't know.

Gladys I thought you might have known something about its history.

Ethel I do. My Barry rented it two months ago.

Gladys I was thinking of a little further back than that. *(She walks across the room, arms outstretched.)* I feel discomfort here.

Ethel I've some Rennies in my bag. Or how about a nice cup of tea?

Gladys There wouldn't be anything a *teeny* bit stronger, would there? I feel the need to stock up on my psychic powers, and a glass of sherry would stoke the fires.

Ethel I doubt there is, Gladys. My Barry's a tea-totaller.

Gladys Really? Do such people actually exist? I'll have to make do with boring tea then... unless there's a drop of rum to pep it up?

Ethel I don't think there will be.

Gladys Pity. I'll be running on half power.

Ethel I'll put the kettle on. *(Exits to the kitchen DL.)*

Gladys *(moving around the room with her arms outstretched)* You know. I definitely sense a soul in torment somewhere in the vicinity. Someone, or something, is crying out for help.

Ethel *(entering)* I don't hear anything.

Gladys But you're not tuned in, are you, Ethel? We are surrounded by waves of energy, but you need special skills to tap into them.

Ethel Or a tele'.

Gladys What do you mean a tele'?

Ethel My Sid explained it to me. I asked him how the programmes got into our tele', and he said they come through the air in waves, just like you said. You can't see them, but they're hitting you all the time. It worries me, I can tell you. You don't know what they're doing to your body, do you? They could even be making you puerile.

Gladys No, these aren't television programmes. Even your Sidney couldn't explain these. And there is definitely a presence trying to make itself heard.

Ethel Barry said it was more like a thumping sound.

Gladys *(excitedly)* You mean, a knocking?
Ethel I suppose so.
Gladys I'm so glad you called me in, Ethel. I have a feeling I can do so much here.
Ethel In that case, we'd best get to work. Barry's given me a list of things to do, like answering the phone, taking messages, and looking after the office.
Gladys But I thought we were here to investigate psychic phenomena.
Ethel I think if he'd asked for what you said, I'd have remembered.
Gladys Where is Barry at this moment?
Ethel He always tells me he's out there pacing the mean streets.
Gladys Ah, the energy of the young. How soon it changes into the frailty of age. Will he be away long?
Ethel He didn't say. He's out with Deirdre and another friend called Sick.
Gladys I envy the young their friendships. Thank goodness I have plenty of friends on the other side.
Ethel You mean across the street?
Gladys What exactly does your son do?
Ethel He sort of looks into things.
Gladys A bit like me, eh?
Ethel You didn't bring your crystal ball, did you?
Gladys Too heavy, but I brought the cards. *(Takes out a set of playing cards and sits at the desk.)*
Ethel It must be lovely to have the gift, Gladys.
Gladys It can be, but sometimes it's a terrible responsibility, especially when I see something that could have awful consequences.
Ethel We used to play that game when Mum and Dad were alive - Consequences - and it *was* pretty awful.
Gladys This is more than a game. There is darkness all around us.
Ethel Oh dear, and I do try to keep the window clean. Shall I put the light on?
Gladys No need. Just pull up a chair to the desk. *(Ethel pulls the straight backed chair up to the desk.)* Now you cut the cards.
Ethel *(picking up the paper knife from the desk)* Won't that ruin them, Gladys?
Gladys I think I'd better do it. *(She cuts the cards and lays some out on the desk.)* Now that is odd.
Ethel What's odd?
Gladys It's very confusing. There seem to be a lot of diamonds here,

The Scent of Danger

	and a dark Queen. Ace of Hearts too, and a Jack of Spades. Does it make any sense to you, Ethel?
Ethel	A dark lady, diamonds, a heart and a Knave? It doesn't say anything to me.
Gladys	*(shivering)* Has it turned cold in here? I feel all shivery.
Ethel	You'll happen be sickening for one of them virals. They're a bit like tele' waves, so my Sid says, floating about in the air ready to pounce.
Gladys	*(shivering again)* Ooh, there it is again.
Ethel	Silly me! The window's open. You're in a draught. *(She closes it.)* There, is that better?
Gladys	Someone must have walked over my grave.
Ethel	It'll be vandals. They're always hanging about the cemetery. What you need is that cup of tea. Kettle should be boiling. *(Exits to kitchen DL.)*
Gladys	*(turning the cards)* I'm getting too old for this. I should take up patience. *(She hears a noise beneath her feet and jumps up. She bends and stares at the floor, listening.)* Did you hear that?
Ethel	*(entering with a tray with two mugs of tea on it which she places on the desk)* Hear what? *(Sits at the desk.)*
Gladys	A sort of dull thud downstairs. Are you sure there is no one in the flat below?
Ethel	So everyone keeps telling me.
Gladys	But if there's no one downstairs…
Ethel	Spooky isn't it?
Gladys	I was right! There is something odd going on.
Ethel	Ooh Gladys, I'm getting a bit scared.
Gladys	I have to admit I'm rather worried too. Usually I have no fear of such things. After all, these are merely people who have gone before.
Ethel	I wish *I'd* gone - before I sat down!
Gladys	We must try and establish contact with this tortured soul.
Ethel	Couldn't we write it a letter?
Gladys	No, it is our duty to lay him or her to rest.
Ethel	I just hope they don't lay *us* to rest first! Shall we sing a lullaby?
Gladys	Courage, friend. We have the power and we must use it.
Ethel	But I only came to take messages.
Gladys	We must try and send messages across the ether.

Ethel	Talking of messages, there's one on Barry's machine.
Gladys	Which machine?
Ethel	The one connected to the phone.
Gladys	Ah, the answering machine. Useful items. I have one of those myself.
Ethel	Is that in case any spirits want to contact you while you're out?
Gladys	Let me see now. No, Ethel, no messages. That red light blinks when there's a message waiting.
Ethel	But there was! It was a man who sounded very angry. He was complaining about his daughter's fingers, as I recall.
Gladys	Perhaps it was our troubled spirit trying to make contact. Anyway, this machine isn't even switched on at the moment.
Ethel	Messages disappearing? It's like that Bermuda Tangle. We'll be next to vanish, Gladys! Barry'll come back and there'll be no one here- just an eerie silence…
Gladys	Pull yourself together, Ethel! You're making *me* nervous!
Ethel	There's something horrible here, isn't there?
Gladys	I believe so. I think a crime was committed here, and the spirits of the victims are still here, tormented and troubled!
Ethel	A bit like me! Ooh Gladys, what do we do?
Gladys	They're trying to contact us. I can feel them desperately seeking a way to speak to us. We are here, spirits! Give us a sign! *(The phone rings. Both women scream and throw their arms around each other.)* Aren't you going to answer it?
Ethel	Suppose… suppose it's… you know… the spirits?
Gladys	*(disengaging herself from Ethel)* I've never known them to use the phone before.
Ethel	*You* answer it, Gladys.
Gladys	*(gingerly picks up the phone.)* Hullo. *(She listens. She doesn't speak, but just puts the phone down again as if in a dream.)*
Ethel	Well? Was it our Barry? What did he say? Come on, Gladys, who was it?
Gladys	It wasn't Barry. It was a man - a very angry man.
Ethel	What did he say?
Gladys	He said when he gets his hands on us, he's going to wring our necks.
Ethel	Ooh, Gladys! What shall we do?
Gladys	I suggest we get out of this office as quickly as possible and find somewhere to hide. I happen to know a place on the other side of town where the landlord will open a bottle of sherry for

The Scent of Danger

two scared old ladies, and no questions asked.
Ethel We can't desert our post just like that.
Gladys Too right we can! I prefer my neck as it is - wrinkled but unwrung!
Ethel *(doubtfully)* I don't know...
(Without warning, the cardboard clock falls over. In an instant, Ethel and Gladys have dashed out, leaving the door open. The phone rings three or four times, then goes silent. There is a slight pause, then Deirdre arrives at the door. She is dressed in skirt and sweater over which is a coat, and her hair is dishevelled. She carries a clothing store carrier bag. She stops on seeing the clock and hauls it upright again on the bed. She takes off her coat and hangs it up on the hatstand. She tests one of the mugs of tea on the desk for warmth and drinks some. She sits at the desk, wearily. Enter Barry from landing.)
Barry Hello, love. You on your own?
Deirdre Place was empty when I arrived, and the door was wide open.
Barry Mum promised to stay and keep an eye on it.
Deirdre I'm absolutely bushed. And I feel very filthy.
Barry Sorry, darling - no time for sex at the moment
Deirdre Ha ha! It's also highly annoying that I'm in this state because of that woman! I shudder to think what goes on at night in those garages we looked at. There were some very strange objects lying around in the rubbish.
Barry The worse thing is, Suzanne's nowhere to be found, vanished - a bit like Mum and Gladys - though mum's scarf and coat are still here.
Deirdre Let's face it, darling, she could be anywhere. It's a big town and you could hide an army in it if you wanted to. We're never going to find her.
Barry We can't give up yet. Think of the money. Think of the cottage, and Wayne and Sharon and Tiddles.
Deirdre All I can think of at the moment is a nice, hot bath.
Barry Be my guest.
Deirdre What? You mean have one here?
Barry There's a perfectly good bathroom through there, with bags of hot water.
Deirdre I couldn't. I mean, not with you in the flat.
Barry I promise not to peek.
Deirdre Even so, I think I should be chaperoned. I mean to say, what if your animal passions got the better of you? *(She indicates*

	he should sit on the desk chair and she sits on his knee.) I mean, what could a weak, defenceless girl like me do against a big, powerful man like you?
Barry	Weak and defenceless, you said?
Deirdre	And I'd be all naked too. Does that conjure up lustful images in your mind, Barry?
Barry	*(looking her up and down)* Not really.
Deirdre	Why not? Don't answer. I know why not. *(She gets off his knee.)* You're too busy thinking about that rich cow, Suzanne, aren't you?
Barry	*(standing and moving C)* It's my *job* to think about her. I'm supposed to be rescuing her - for a fee. *(Bitterly.)* So far, I haven't even found her rotten cat! That's how useless I am at this detective lark. I should pack it all in and get a proper job, like you said.
Deirdre	*(going to him)* Oh, no, Barry. I didn't mean… I think you're a brill detective, honest. I have every confidence in you.
Barry	You're the only one. What's the betting dear old Rick finds her first and ends up with the reward *and* the girl.
Deirdre	I doubt it. I haven't seen sight nor sound of Ricky boy all morning. I thought he was supposed to be combing the streets.
Barry	Funny that. You'd have thought we'd have bumped into him at some point.
Deirdre	I bet he's gone off cabbying.
Barry	Even you vanished for half an hour at one point.
Deirdre	A girl has to go sometime, you know.
Barry	Anyway, you have your bath. It's OK. I'm going back out.
Deirdre	I'll come with you.
Barry	No, you've done enough. I'll tell you what, Deirdre, you've been far more help to me than my so-called mate, or even my family. And I appreciate it, I really do.
Deirdre	That's 'cause I love you, Barry.
Barry	I'm sure I'd get on better if I could find my hat. It wasn't lying in the gutter outside like it usually is.
Deirdre	I think you look like a real private eye in that hat.
Barry	It's disappeared as completely as my mother.
Deirdre	Maybe she's been kidnapped too.
Barry	Don't. I've enough on my plate at the moment.
Deirdre	You take care, love. Don't wear your little self out. *(She exits to bathroom DR, taking the carrier with her.)*

The Scent of Danger

Barry   *(sighing)* Right. *(In American accent.)* Hank Silver could hear the clock ticking away the minutes of Layla's captivity. He wondered how she was bearing up under the strain. He knew she was a tough cookie, but would she crumble under torture? Torture? Surely her captors wouldn't harm that delicate skin, that oh so luscious body?

Sidney   *(enters from the landing.)* You're surely not talking about your mother, are you, Barry? No, of course you're not!

Barry   Oh, hi, Dad. Mum's not here. I don't know where she's got to.

Sidney   Not here? That's good, son. It'll give us a clear run.

Barry   A clear run?

Sidney   You know. A session of Countdown. You promised.

Barry   Dad, I really have a lot on at this moment...

Sidney   Not going back on your promise to your own father, are you? To the father who loaned you the money that got you out of a certain spot of trouble...?

Barry   Oh, what the heck! I'm never going to find Suzanne anyway. Let Rick have her - and the money! *(Hangs his coat on the stand.)*

Sidney   Suzanne? I thought you were committed to that Deirdre woman? Don't say you're sowing wild oats, Barry. Your mother would never forgive you.

Barry   It's OK. Suzanne is Rick's girl friend. I was just looking for her.

Sidney   He can't be much of a man if he's had to hire you to find his girlfriend.

Barry   It's complicated.

Sidney   Tell me something new! *Any* dealings with women are never simple. Right, are we ready?

Barry   Not really. That clock doesn't work for one thing.

Sidney   It doesn't have to, lad. It's just there so I can get over any feelings of inhibition I might have. Can we lift it over here? I'm going to be sitting behind the desk, so it should be behind me to get the best effect. *(They manhandle the clock across and prop it up against the window on the desk.)* Now the box. *(Places the cardboard box on the floor near the desk.)*

Barry   Who am I playing? Richard Whiteley?

Sidney   You'll have to be Carol, seeing as how we've no one to dig out the letters. Now, you know what happens, don't you?

Barry   I think so. You choose consonants and vowels and try to make the longest word you can from the letters.

Sidney   I'll sit at the desk. *(He does so.)* Have you got pen and paper?

Barry	Should be on the desk.
Sidney	Right. Vowel.
Barry	*(picking from the box)* A.
Sidney	Consonant.
Barry	Z.
Sidney	I don't like that. Can I have another?
Barry	You won't be allowed another on the real show.
Sidney	Oh, well…Consonant.
Barry	N.
Sidney	Vowel.
Barry	E.
Sidney	Consonant.
Barry	N.
Sidney	Consonant.
Barry	S.
Sidney	Last one. Vowel.
Barry	U. And you have thirty seconds starting - now!
Sidney	Could you hum the music to keep up the pressure?
Barry	I'm not wasting valuable time humming. I'll just tell you when thirty seconds is up. Half has gone already.
Sidney	Couldn't you start the clock again?
Barry	No I couldn't. You wanted to know what pressure was like. Ten seconds.
Sidney	Er…Zen…Ens…
Barry	Time's up.
Sidney	Are you sure that was thirty seconds?
Barry	A little over.
Sidney	It was the letters. You gave me a rotten selection of letters.
Barry	*You* chose them.
Sidney	I bet you didn't shuffle them before you took them out.
Barry	I didn't. They came off the top as you packed them in the box.
Sidney	All right, clever dick! *You* make a word out of them.
Barry	*(sighing)* I'm sure if you couldn't do it with all your training, I'll be no good. *(As he speaks, he kneels and arranges the letters on the floor.)* Oh, my goodness!
Sidney	You've made a word?
Barry	Yes.
Sidney	Using all the letters?
Barry	Yes.

The Scent of Danger

Sidney I bet it's not a real word. Let me have a look. *(He gets up and comes over to Barry.)* I knew it! You're not allowed proper names! That spells 'Suzanne'. You're disqualified.

Barry Sorry, Dad, I've just got to go. I know I promised, but this is important. This is a sign to remind me it's not a game any more.

Sidney It's just a game to me.

Barry I mean this job I've taken on. If I'm going to get anywhere in this world, I can't give in just because I'm hungry and tired. Hank Silver wouldn't give in. He'd rather die in the attempt.

Sidney I thought your mate's name was Rick?

Barry Hank is the one who inspires me.

Sidney We all need our heroes, son. Mine's Nicholas Parsons. *(Barry sniffs the air, then bends and sniffs near the floor.)* Sorry, Barry. *(Sidney inspects the soles of his shoes.)* Didn't see it. Damn dogs- this town's a wall-to-wall toilet for animals!

Barry *(straightening up)* It's not that sort of smell. This is quite nice. I've smelt it before, and not so long ago either. *(He stands.)* It's given me an idea. Dad, would you keep an eye on things here for me?

Sidney Of course I will. I'll be your second- in- command. I'll man the comms link. Are you connected to the Internet, son?

Barry I'm only just connected to Directory Enquiries, Dad! And fancy you knowing about the Inter… but, of course, I forgot. The quizzes. You know about everything.

Sidney Not quite. If I live to be a hundred, I'll never understand your mother.

Barry I really think I'm onto something at last.

Sidney Then you go get 'em, kid! *(Barry exits to landing.)* Let's get some light in here. *(Sidney takes down the clock from in front of the window and props it against wall R.)* That's better. *(He sits down at the desk, takes off his cap and puts on the headphones, and pulls the angle poise lamp down in front of his face like a microphone. He takes hold of the games console joystick.)* Red Leader to Tower. Red Leader to Tower. Are you receiving me? Over. *(He cups his hands round his mouth.)* Tower to Red Leader. You are coming in too fast. Throttle back! I repeat -throttle back! Over. *(Into lamp.)* Sorry, Tower. No can do. Flaps shot to hell. Fuselage leaking like a jolly old sieve. Afraid this is going to be a sticky landing. Over. *(Hands over mouth.)* Tower to Red Leader. Do your best, old son. It's all your country can ask of you in its darkest hour.

ACT II

Good luck, old bean. Over. *(Into lamp.)* It's no good, Tower. Engine's on fire. Wings have fallen off, and the cockpit's ablaze. At least I got twenty of the swine before I pranged. I can see the tower dead ahead. I'll use my last ounce of energy to swerve and miss you, but it'll be a damn close thing. Still, good to know my last view of dear old Blighty will be your anxious faces peering through the glass... *(Barry's face appears at the window. Sidney jumps.)* Ruddy hell, Barry! What are you trying to do? Give me a heart attack?
(Barry motions him to open the window. Sidney does so and Barry climbs in.)

Barry Thanks, Dad.

Sidney *(taking off the headphones.)* Have doors gone out of fashion all of sudden?

Barry Sorry about that. I think I've solved one of my cases. It was all down to my hat, you see.

Sidney It's what's *under* your hat that bothers me! Have you been overdoing it?

Barry *(pacing)* When I threw my hat out of the window earlier...

Sidney You chucked your hat out of the window? For no reason? You'd best sit down, lad. You're obviously having some sort of breakdown. It was all in that medical dictionary I was swotting up the other day. It's down to the strain of modern living...

Barry Will you listen? It was an accident. I'm always doing it. Usually my hat goes straight into the gutter for Mum to pick up...

Sidney Oh, you do it for your mother's benefit, do you? That's all right then.

Barry This time, the wind must have caught it and blown it somewhere else. The flat below this is empty, and below this window is another, bigger, one. And, most importantly, it's got a broken pane near the top.

Sidney You haven't been throwing stones at the windows, have you? I don't know what to say, Barry. Me and your mother have tried to bring you up right...

Barry *(sitting on the edge of the desk)* Dad! Will you please listen? The curtains downstairs were closed, so I couldn't see in from the street level. But where the window was broken at the top, the wind must have pushed them apart a little way. And that caravan you hate so much came in very useful. I climbed on top of it...

Sidney Look, Barry, I'd have bought you a new hat, if you'd asked. There was no need to risk life and limb...

The Scent of Danger

Barry And when I looked in, I could see my hat lying in the corner of the front room down there.

Sidney And I'm right glad you spotted it, seeing as how it means so much to you.

Barry *(moving C)* The other thing I saw lying on the floor in there was a cat. It had either been drugged or it was dead.

Sidney Chances are you killed it with your flying hat! Has it got a metal rim like in that Bond film?

Barry It was a black cat, with a bent ear, one white paw, and a white patch on its nose.

Sidney Why don't you go look in a pet shop for a cat, like normal people?

Barry Don't you see? It's the cat I've been looking for. I'm going back down there and break in.

Sidney Honest, son. Pullins will be open now, and their door'll be unlocked. What say I take you down there and let you have the pick of the stock? I'll even pay for it, if you're so desperate.

Barry Sorry, it has to be this one. And I've a feeling there'll be more than a cat and a hat in there.

Sidney *(patronisingly)* Yes, son. There'll very likely be a mat, and even a rat - not to mention a certain prat!

Barry When I was arranging those letters on the floor...

Sidney And cheating.

Barry And cheating, there was a faint smell of perfume drifting up through the floorboards - a very expensive perfume, worn by a certain young lady.

Sidney More likely to be your mother's carpet shampoo. And you took a liking to this perfume did you?

Barry Naturally. I'm only human, after all.

Sidney While we're out getting the cat, we'll nip into Boots and get you a bottle - though *you'll* have to ask for it. I don't know! You'll be wanting your ears pierced next!

Barry Will you keep a look out again? Just watch from the window, and if anyone comes down the street, give us a shout.

Sidney Oh my God! I've always wanted to get on television and now I'm going to get my wish - chief suspect on Crimewatch!

Barry It'll be OK, honest. I'll just get a knife.

Sidney You're not going to dissect the flaming animal, are you?

Barry To force the lock downstairs.

Sidney Have you got a credit card?

Barry Dad, we haven't time to go shopping.

ACT II

Sidney I mean for breaking into houses.
Barry Are you a secret burglar? *(Searches his pockets.)*
Sidney It's your mother. She keeps leaving the house keys inside when we go out. I've got quite adept with our flexible friend. Would you like me to go and open it for you?
Barry No, thanks. If there are going to be any arrests, best it be me. Ah, got one! I shan't be long.
Sidney I'll just sit here and listen out for police sirens.
Barry Oh, I nearly forgot. Will you see if you can locate Deirdre? Haven't set eyes on her for ages.
Sidney Deirdre? That nice, easy-going lass? You can't have ... I mean, a cat's understandable - never could stand the things myself - but your own girlfriend?
Barry What are you on about? She's probably just dead to the world in the bath. See you later. *(Exits to landing.)*
Sidney Dead in the bath? Oh, no! It's getting like 10 Rillington Place. I can't take much more of this - dead cats, drowned fiancées, missing wives! Ethel! Where's my Ethel? And Gladys is missing too. He wouldn't... he couldn't have... *(He takes a deep breath.)* Steel yourself, Sid, lad. Pretend you're facing the producers for the very first interview. *(He walks towards exit DR.)* Name? Sidney Bigley. Occupation? Father of a serial killer! Oh Lord! *(He exits DR. Off.)* Ethel? Deirdre? Is anybody still alive out here? *(Deirdre gives a piercing scream off.)* Sorry, love. Didn't mean to catch you 'au naturel', so to speak. I thought you were dead. *(He emerges backwards out of the doorway, his hands over his eyes.)* Name? Sidney Bigley. Occupation? Peeping Tom! *(He collapses into the desk chair.)* My poor heart won't take much more of this. One more shock and I'm six feet under for sure.
(There is a noise out on the landing. Sidney leaps to his feet. Enter Suzanne. She is grubby and her clothing is crumpled. She is very angry. She is pulling the last of a length of rope from around her wrists. Barry follows her in, hesitantly.)
Suzanne A whole night it's taken you to find me! I've been tied up in a cold, dark, damp cupboard for hours and hours! Call yourself a private eye? You must have had it firmly shut if you couldn't detect that I was being held right under your feet! You incompetent, useless... arrgh! Words fail me! Where's your phone?
Barry On the desk.
(Sidney mutely signals 'who she?' to Barry. Barry just shrugs.)

The Scent of Danger

Suzanne *(at the desk, dialling)* Hello? I want a taxi right away. *(To Barry.)* Where are we? Or aren't you too sure about that either?
Barry Flat 2, Brinsley Mansions.
Suzanne *(into phone)* Flat 2, Brinsley Mansions. To go to Snaresby Manor. Right away. Thank you. *(To Barry.)* I'm getting out of this madhouse as fast as I can. *(Dials again.)*
Sidney *(to Barry, quietly)* Let me get this straight. She's come from downstairs?
Barry That's right.
Sidney So, she must be the cat you saw down there? Are we into witchcraft now?
Barry Your imagination's running riot.
Sidney It's hardly surprising, what's been going on round here!
Suzanne *(to Barry)* You've even managed to lose my cat again.
Barry That's not my fault. It took off like a bat out of hell as soon as it came to. Or should that be a cat out of hell?
Suzanne *(into phone)* Hello? Daddykins? *(Her voice turns babyish.)* Yes, it's your wittle Suzie, safe, but only just. I've been through hell, Daddy, sheer hell! You've got to get the police right away. Tell them to surround Brinsley Mansions in the centre of town and arrest everyone inside, especially a man with an Italian accent.
Barry Italian? That wouldn't be my landlord, would it?
Sidney Your landlord? I might have known it!
Barry You can't have us arrested.
Sidney What do you mean 'us?' I'm totally innocent of anything.
Suzanne Oh, my father's a magistrate. Don't worry, he'll think of something you can be charged with! He's in favour of bringing back hanging. *(Into phone.)* Yes, I'm still here, Daddy. I'll be home soon. I've ordered a cab - no, it's all right. It'll be quicker. The police can interview me at home.
Barry Ask him about the ransom.
Suzanne Who's with me, Daddy? Just some passing lunatic! Daddy, you haven't given any of your hard-earned money to that horrible man, have you... ? You have? An hour ago? Where did you leave it... ? At the tax office? And they've kept it? How did they know... oh, your name was on the holdall and they did some checking. *(Sidney chuckles.)* And you can wipe that grin off your face. No, not you, Daddy. I'm well aware you have nothing to grin about. But you have always paid your taxes on

ACT II

time, haven't you...? Ah, I see. Poor Daddykins. Employing a corrupt accountant on top of everything else. What's that, Daddy...? Cutbacks? Not my allowance, surely? Can't we discuss this when I get home? Love to Mummy. Bye. *(She replaces the phone and sits in chair.)* This is a nightmare.

Barry Would you like a cup of tea?

Sidney My Ethel swears by a cup of tea.

Suzanne I do not want a cup of lousy tea! All I want to do is get out of here as soon as I can, and get back to civilisation.

Sidney Now just a minute, young lady. We're as civilised as...

Suzanne You call kidnapping 'civilised'?

Sidney We didn't kidnap anyone. For all I know, my own wife has been kidnapped too.

Suzanne Oh yeah? And who's to say you weren't involved in mine? I'm sure you could use an extra few pounds for your bingo or whatever you get up to for enjoyment.

Sidney Now just a minute, young lady! For a start, I'd be grateful if you'd stop speaking to me as if I've crawled out from under a stone! From what I gather, my lad's the one responsible for setting you free from whatever you got yourself into...

Suzanne Got myself into? *(She stands.)* I didn't do anything. Last night, on my way to my car after my aromatherapy session, I was grabbed, tied up, gagged and thrown into a filthy caravan. I was then driven here, where I was imprisoned in a cupboard so small I could hardly breathe. Naturally I struggled, but there were two of them, that Italian and someone wearing a mask. Perhaps that was one of you?

Barry What time was this?

Suzanne I don't know. Around ten thirty, I think.

Barry Couldn't have been me. At that time, I was ankle deep in cow dung near your home, looking for your cat.

Sidney And I was at home with Ethel, having my nightly cocoa.

Suzanne All right! It was someone else, then. Anyway, I ended up right underneath your feet. I was let out once to use the bathroom. Other than that, I was tied up so tight, my circulation was nearly cut off. I could move one foot slightly, and I kicked and kicked at that cupboard door, but you're obviously deaf as well as stupid!

Sidney But even so...

Suzanne And to add insult to injury, they brought me to this very office first. The ransom note was typed on your typewriter! He seemed to get a kick out of thinking that, if the note was

The Scent of Danger

traced, you'd be a suspect.
Sidney The cheeky beggar!
Barry I *knew* if I'd got a look at that ransom note, I'd have solved it.
Sidney I doubt you'd have suspected yourself, son. Anyway, young lady, whatever you say, if it wasn't for Barry here, you'd still be locked up. So show a bit of gratitude.
Suzanne Gratitude?
Sidney A simple 'thank you' will do.
Suzanne *(teeth gritted)* I wouldn't thank him if he was the last person on earth! And where's that bloody taxi?!
Sidney Just because you've got money doesn't mean you can treat us like dirt.
Suzanne Oh, that's precisely what it does do!
Sidney In that case, I'll just have to take you over my knee and teach you some manners. That's how we dealt with naughty children before the world went mad.
Suzanne You wouldn't dare! I'd have you for assault! The police would lock you up and throw away the key.
Sidney Do you know, it would be worth it, just to teach you a lesson in manners.
Suzanne You're all barking!
Sidney *(moving threateningly towards her)* Well? How about a word of gratitude?
Suzanne *(defeated)* Oh, what the hell! I'm too weak and tired to argue any more. All right - thank you, Barry. Now, let me out of here!
Sidney I'll see if your cab's coming. *(He looks out of the window.)* At least that caravan's not blocking the pavement any more, Barry.
Barry No?
Sidney No. It's off down the street like its wheels are on fire.
Barry What? That'll be Salini, making a run for it! *(Dashes out onto the landing.)*
Sidney He'll never catch it on foot. Oh, here's someone pulling up now.
Suzanne Thank goodness. I can't bear these filthy clothes one minute more. *(She is nearly in tears.)* I'm not used to this sort of treatment. I'm used to nice things, and home comforts, and people who appreciate me... Oh, Mr. Bigley! It was awful! I was so scared!
(Sidney goes and puts an arm around her, handing over a large hanky.)

Sidney It's OK, love. I know you've been through a lot. In fact, I have to admire your courage. A lot of young *blokes* I know wouldn't have stood up to being treated like you were.
Suzanne Despite what you said earlier?
Sidney Let's just say that I don't believe you're as selfish as you like to make out.
Suzanne *(dabbing her eyes)* You - you won't tell anyone I've been crying?
Sidney What? And ruin your reputation? 'Course not!
(Enter Barry from landing. He is supporting Ethel and Gladys. They are both under the influence and giggling madly.)
Barry Look what I found falling out of Rick's cab.
Gladys Where is the dear boy? I've got the fare here.
Sidney *(rushing to Ethel)* You're alive!
Ethel I'll say, Sidney. I haven't been this alive for years!
Barry Where have you been?
Ethel Gladys knew this little place where we could hide. Sells a smashing drop of sherry. But don't tell Lilly Law, will you?
(Enter Rick from landing. He stops when he sees Suzanne.)
Rick Oh, hi, Suze! You're safe! Thank God!
Suzanne Don't you 'hi Suze' me, you rat! Where were you last night when I needed you?
Rick Er, sorry, doll. Urgent appointment.
Barry Here, Rick can run you home, Suzanne, seeing as how he's here.
Suzanne *(dangerously)* You don't think I'd trust him ever again do you?
Rick Right, Suze - just as you say. Well, if I'm not needed... Er, I'd best be off.
Gladys Your fare, young man.
Ethel No, he's not - he's dark!
Rick *(backing towards the door)* Forget it, ladies. Happy to be of service. Oh, by the way, I've tied your dog up downstairs.
Barry What dog? We haven't got a dog.
Rick You have now. Your mother made me stop and pick it up. It was hanging about near the chemist.
Barry Mum, what have you done?
Ethel But he looked so hungry, Barry.
Barry I suppose I'll have to take it back.
Rick I'll see you some time. *(Exits to landing.)*
Sidney *(at window)* Taxi's here, love.

The Scent of Danger

Suzanne Thank goodness! *(To Sidney.)* Goodbye, Mr. Bigley.
Suzanne Goodbye, and you take care now.
Barry Do you want me to see you home?
Suzanne From now on, I'm looking after myself! *(Exits to landing.)*
Barry You'd better sit down before you fall down, Mum.
Ethel Good idea, son! Sorry we didn't stay to man the barricades. We had a pressing need to get out of here.
(Ethel and Gladys collapse on the bed.)
Sidney Just look at the state of you, Ethel.
Gladys We simply had need of a spot of Dutch courage, didn't we?
Ethel S'right - to see off the ghosts. And it worked. Can't see any ghosts now, can you, Gladys?
Gladys *(waving her hand about)* I can't even see my own fingers.
Ethel And my teeth are itching something chronic.
Sidney Ghosts? Boozing? I don't know, Barry. You live with someone for thirty years and you still don't understand them.
Barry I'm just pleased they're safe. I hadn't realised what danger I left them in. If that Salini had come back, it doesn't bear thinking about.
Ethel I can take care of myself! *(She has put on a balaclava with two eye holes.)* Stick 'em up, buster!
Barry Where did you get that?
Ethel *(taking it off)* Found it under the seat in old Sicky's cab. He must have copied the one you used to wear at school, Barry. See, I told you the others'd envy you one day.
Gladys I can't think why that Ricky would want to cover his face up. I found him rather fanciable myself. If I'd been able to control my hands, I'd have given his knee a squeeze.
Ethel *(nudging her)* I'd have squeezed more than his knee, given half the chance!
Sidney Ethel!
Ethel There's life in the old dog yet.
Gladys Which is more than can be said for that cat.
Barry Which cat?
Ethel The black one with the bent ear. Sick had to swerve to miss a lunatic pulling a caravan, and this cat sort of got in the way.
Gladys It's all right, Ethel. I saw it limping off down Banner Street. He must have just winged it.
Barry Poor Cleopatra! It's been through more than any of us. *(He crosses to bed and picks up the balaclava.)* You shouldn't

	have pinched Rick's balaclava though, Mum.
Gladys	We told you. With his looks, he didn't need it.
Ethel	I just thought our Barry might need it more. Oh, nearly forgot, Sid. We stopped off at the house. There was a letter for you. *(She takes it out of her pocket and gives it to him.)*
Barry	I still don't see what Rick would want with a balaclava.
Sidney	Search me, unless he's started robbing banks.
Barry	Just a minute. The driver of that black car I saw at the Manor looked like he had his face covered up. And I've been mulling over the fact that Rick was supposed to meet Suzanne last night, but he said he'd forgotten.
Sidney	It'd be hard to forget someone like her, son.
Barry	Exactly! I ran into a mate of ours while I was in town earlier - Harry - and he never said anything about any all-night drinking session with Rick. Surely he'd have mentioned something like that, wouldn't he?
Sidney	Hang on, son! Is this my starter for ten? *(Ethel and Gladys have fallen asleep leaning on each other.)*
Barry	Suppose Rick was in on the kidnap? Maybe it was him who stole her cat. He was always a big spender, and Suzanne has stacks of money. What if he took the cat intending to hold it to ransom? Only he couldn't demand much for a cat, could he? Whereas, if he took Suzanne herself... But he needs somewhere to hide her. Enter Luigi Salini with an empty flat and a love of easy money. Rick would get a real kick out of her being held under my nose while he sends us off on a wild goose chase all over town. And I bet the Porsche is hidden in his garage!
Sidney	Just as well she didn't take up your suggestion of going home with Rick.
Barry	God, I'm stupid! I nearly gave him a second chance! I should pack this detective work in.
Sidney	I think the time has come to pass on this information to the police, son.
Barry	You're right. Especially as I'm not now getting a lousy bean for all my work. *(He sighs.)* That won't please Deirdre. And talking of Deirdre, where on earth is she?
Sidney	Ah, I'm sorry about that, Barry. It was a genuine mistake, believe me. I'll tell you one thing in confidence, though. When you finally get to see her without all those drab clothes she normally wears, you're in for a very pleasant surprise.
Barry	Dad! You don't mean you've seen her...

The Scent of Danger

Sidney As the day she was born, son, and it wasn't the worse sight of my life by a long chalk. There's more to that lass than meets the eye!
Barry But where is she?
Sidney It's a rare place for vanishing, is this flat.
Barry Aren't you going to open your letter?
Sidney It'll be a bill. *(He opens it.)* Oh, I must sit down!
Barry What is it?
Sidney I've got an audition in three weeks time - for 'Wheel of Fortune'!
Barry That's wonderful! Well done, Dad! Mum! Dad's going to be on TV at last.
(Gladys and Ethel snore on.)
Sidney *(panicking)* I'd best get preparing, Barry. I shall need a dirty great lit-up wheel fitting in the floor here by the desk. And then there's the wall of letters... *(Carries on planning.)*
Deirdre *(Off)* Cooee! Barry, darling!
Barry Deirdre? Are you all right?
(Deirdre enters from bathroom. She has undergone an amazing transformation. She wears a tight, low-cut dress, makeup, and her hair has been done. She moves seductively across stage from R to L, humming the guitar intro. from 'Layla' by Derek and the Dominos.)
Barry Deirdre? Is that really you?
Deirdre Yes, sweetheart. Sorry it took so long, but makeup is devilish difficult to apply when your eyesight isn't all it should be. And I wanted to be just perfect for my Barry.
Barry Mum! Gladys! Look at Deirdre! Isn't she absolutely gorgeous?
(Ethel and Gladys snore on.)
Deirdre *(pausing C and posing.)* Do you really think so?
Barry I do. And you look so different without your glasses.
Deirdre I've decided to try and manage without them from now on.
Barry At last! I've found my dream girl! Layla, will you marry me? *(Holds out his arms.)*
Deirdre Hank, my darling! Of course I will! *(She holds out her arms and moves across centre stage and throws them around the coats on the stand.)* Ooh, Barry, love! You'll have to give this detective work up. You haven't half lost weight!
(Lights fade. Curtain.)

Properties
ACT I Scene 1
Desk under window L *(on it)* manual typewriter - telephone and answering machine - working angle poise lamp - empty In and Out trays - games console joystick - paper knife - pair of binoculars - pair of hi-fi headphones - blank A4 paper - cards with phone number printed on - pen - notebook. *(under it)* waste paper bin
Single bed UR *(on it)* sheets - pillow - counterpane or duvet
Bedside cabinet to R of rear door *(on it)* small working bedside lamp
Filing cabinet to L of rear door *(optional)*
Upright chair against wall DL
Coffee table C *(on it)* magazines
OFF landing 6' diameter cardboard clock

Personal
Barry   trench coat - trilby hat - money *(for Luigi)*
Ethel   coat - headscarf - vacuum cleaner - Barry's hat - duster
Sidney   flat cap - cardboard box containing cardboard letters A, Z, N, E, N, S, U in that order
Deirdre   spectacles - duffel coat or similar - scarf - woolly hat - two carriers containing groceries
Suzanne   set of car keys

ACT I Scene 2
Personal
Luigi   gun
Rick   black clothing - balaclava with eyeholes

ACT I Scene 3
Personal
Ethel   coat - headscarf - vacuum cleaner

ACT II
Barry's clothes on chair at foot of bed
Personal
Barry   pyjamas - comb - credit card
Ethel   coat - headscarf - vacuum cleaner - tray with two mugs of tea
Gladys   pack of playing cards
Deirdre   coat - clothing store carrier bag
Suzanne   short length of rope
Sidney   large handkerchief
Ethel   Rick's balaclava - letter in envelope

Lighting
ACT I Scene 1
Darkened stage on Curtain up. Light behind panel in glass door. Barry switches bedside light on.
Full lights *(cue)* Ethel switches overhead light on
Overhead and bedside lights off *(cue)* Barry switches off the lights, then exits to landing, closing and locking the door.
At end of scene, fade landing light to indicate passing of time.
ACT I Scene 2
Fade up landing light.
Desk lamp on *(cue)* Luigi switches on the desk light.
Desk lamp off *(cue)* Luigi switches off the desk light.
At end of scene, fade landing light to indicate passing of time.
ACT I Scene 3
Fade up landing light.
Bedside lamp on *(cue)* Barry enters, switches on bedside lamp, then, yawning, moves C.
Desk lamp on *(cue)* Barry goes to desk, switches on desk light and sits down.
At end of scene, all lights fade.
ACT II
Full lighting as for a sunny morning in winter.
Desk light, bedside lamp and landing light off.
At end of Act, all lights fade to black.

Effects
ACT I Scene 1
Knock on landing door (cue) **Ethel**: …so he's going to learn as much as he can.
ACT I Scene 2 *Nil*
ACT I Scene 3
At opening of scene, phone rings twice, then Barry's recorded message is heard on answer machine followed by upper class voice leaving message.
Faint tapping noise
(cue) **Barry** … But all he was left with was the ghost of her presence.
Single loud thump
(cue) **Barry** … you're tired that's all. A good night's sleep and…
Faint tapping (cue) Barry throws his jacket on the bed and unbuckles his

belt
Loud thump
(cue) **Barry** ...Rick? Is that you messing about?
Loud thump
(cue) **Barry** ...Are the Mafia using robots now?
At end of scene, muffled thumping as lights fade, followed by silence.

ACT II

As Act opens, loud knocking on door.
Barry's recorded message on answer machine
(cue) **Ethel** I wonder if Barry knows his phone flashes?
Upper class voice message on answer machine
(cue) **Ethel** I just heard your voice. *(She pushes buttons on answer machine.)*
Knock on landing door
(cue) **Ethel** ...not that I had much of a plan. *(Gladys knocks on the door.)*
Dull thud
(cue) **Gladys** I'm getting too old for this. I should take up patience.
Phone rings
(cue) **Gladys** We are here spirits! Give us a sign!
Phone rings three or four times then goes silent *(cue)* *(In an instant, Ethel and Gladys have dashed out leaving the door open)*
(Suggested theme music for play: 'Layla' by Derek and the Dominoes.)

Other NTP Plays by Michael Park
All of the Monkeys
Feeding The Ducks
Granny's Game
A Hint Of Old World Charm
Luck Be A Lady
The Scent Of Danger
Ten Pence For The Swear Box
A Touch Of Familiarity
Two Purple Gloves
A Wisp Of Scotch Mist

The only monthly magazine passionate about amateur theatre

subscribe online:
www.asmagazine.co.uk

Scan the QR Code to join us on Facebook

Follow us on twitter @amateurstage

www.ingramcontent.com/pod-product-compliance
Lightning Source LLC
Chambersburg PA
CBHW061509040426
42450CB00008B/1532